The Third Coming

Inner Journey
Rt. 1 Box 1966
Sunrise Beach, Missouri 65079

Jim Rosemergy

The Third Coming
©2000 by Jim Rosemergy

Published by Inner Journey
Printed in the United States of America

For information contact:
Jim Rosemergy at Inner Journey

http://www.innerjourney.org

Cover design by Gail Ishmael
Author photo by Ken Clark

Library of Congress Cataloging Data

Library of Congress Control Number: 00-135918
ISBN 0-945175-12-4

The
Third Coming

DEDICATION

The Third Coming is dedicated to the seeds cast by the Tree of Life. These wayshowers gave their lives for humanity knowing that the day would come when we, too, would awaken. Today is the day.

Table of Contents

Author's Note
A New Myth

A friend, Allen Liles, proposed the title of this book. He told me that he had no strong ideas about the content of the book, only the title. The third coming intrigued me. It presupposed that there was a first and second coming. Immediately, I thought of the second coming of Jesus for which most of the Christian world is waiting. Obviously, the first coming has occurred. Jesus lived and promised he would return, but most of the world believes the second coming has not yet happened. Since my initial conversation with Allen, I have discovered that the second coming is not solely a Christian belief. The return of a god-like being is prevalent in many cultures and in other religions.

But what of the third coming? Is it possible that this idea could be relevant for the human family?

For years I have believed that spiritual principles must apply to all human beings regardless of religion. In fact, spiritual things must apply to those who have forsaken religion or even God. However, the things of Spirit must be spiritually discerned. Often, in order to see with the eyes of Spirit, we have to forsake the path trod by the masses and open ourselves to new ideas and revelations. This is the way it has always been. Someone, often a clergy member who is not a ruling member of the sect or a person without religious credentials, has a direct experience of God. The experience is so profound and real that even though it may challenge past beliefs, it is believed to be true, and it is acted upon.

Writing *The Third Coming* has opened my eyes. It began the first evening I sat to meditate upon the mysterious idea of the third coming. In quiet reflection, I saw a kind of vision that I share with you as a myth. It was the way it started for me, so I thought it appropriate to make it our beginning.

> *Long ago there was only one tree, the Tree of Life, the First One, the Only One. Mysteriously, seemingly at random times, it casts a seed upon the ground, once every thousand years or on rare occasions two seeds in a century. Over the course of its eternal existence, the Tree of Life would cast a small number of seeds upon the soil. Either these seeds would multiply and bear fruit, or life would perish from the earth.*
>
> *The good news is that the seeds were wise. They longed for the light, but they first reached down into the darkness of the earth. Their roots ventured inward and deep until they found a spring of eternal, living water. The Tree of Life then knew Its saplings would survive the mighty storms of men and those who would seek to destroy the young trees from within. Each seed became a powerful and fruitful expression of the Tree of Life.*
>
> *Each seed beget thousands of seedlings. At first a nearby hillside was covered. More trees began to grow. Some bore fruit, some did not, but eventually the offspring of the Tree of Life covered the whole earth.*

The First One remained, but now It was not the Only One, and yet it was.

    I am tempted to interpret the myth for you, but I have decided not to do so. Perhaps you understand the symbols of the Tree of Life and Its seeds or perhaps you do not. At this point, understanding is not important. However, your willingness to consider a new myth is vital. Without willingness, you will never come to see the Tree of Life as God, Allah, Yahweh, the First One, the Only One. You will never see the seeds cast by the Tree of Life as Jesus, Buddha, Moses, or Mohammed. You see how I am? I had to give you a hint, but as you will see as you read *The Third Coming*, the myth is only the beginning.

Introduction

I wonder if there is common ground between the many God-ordained religions of the world: Hinduism, Buddhism, Judaism, Christianity, Zoroastrianism, etc. The founders of these religions were spiritual giants who not only walked on earth and occasionally on water, they walked with God. They experienced the Creator and tirelessly gave themselves to a divine plan. I wonder if they had a common purpose? If the followers of every religion were transported back in time to the moment of their religion's conception, would the people discover that they are joined with every other religion in a unity of purpose?

Each founder spoke and acted from his culture. Those who followed tried to capture the heart of the beginning and the soul of the founder, so they could carry the message into the future. Institutions and structure grew. What was once simple became complex. What was once one person caring for another or a man in search of his God became a creed to be spoken and rules to be followed. Sacred sites where God spoke or where a divine power was unleashed became tourist attractions.

I believe the same divine plan was given to each founder of the mighty religions of the world. I am no expert in comparative religions, but I do believe in common sense. If there is only one God, it is logical to assume that there is only one divine plan. What if we could discover it and dedicate ourselves to its expression? What would the world become? These questions are answered in the chapters that follow.

The Third Coming is a different kind of book. I trust that more books like this one will be written, for it explores the common ground that all religions trod. As you read the book, you will find ideas that are in opposition to what you have heard, been taught, or always believed. In some instances, beliefs that have stood unchallenged for centuries will be put to the test. Nothing is taken for granted. The religions that have evolved on our planet have spawned many believers, but also many atheists. These individuals once were open, eager explorers. Then they discovered "the way it is," and they concluded if this is the way God is, what God does, and what I am to do, I want nothing to do with it. And so they turned from God. The tragedy is not that a person turns from a religion or even that he turns from God. The tragedy is that he is no longer an explorer of spiritual things.

This is true of the atheist, but it is also true of the believer. Once a believer *knows* the truth, he is no longer an explorer. He becomes a defender of the faith. He finds safety in those who believe as he believes and in creeds and dogma that reinforce the truth that he now knows. Not all defenders of the faith are without merit. They ground those who venture into uncharted territory. They are stable and trustworthy. They provide a place to test new ideas. However, now is the time for exploration. With telescopes we have turned our attention to our origin as if it began with the birth of a primordial atom or a big bang. Let us mount our own expedition into the kingdom of God in search not of an atom or a sound but of light and the common purpose given to all those who have walked with God.

Section One

The First Coming

Chapter One

Many Wayshowers
Many Missions?

Another Possibility

A group of believers gathered on a hill. According to their leader, this was the appointed time. Jesus would return on this day. They had forsaken the world. There was no longer any need to participate in its madness. In a few short hours, they would be judged and found worthy to dwell in peace and in the presence of God. The men, women, and children brought with them only enough food and water to sustain them as they waited. They sat, they stood, they paced, but always with periodic upward glances. He said he would come out of the clouds.

The day passed and then the night. No Jesus, no second coming. What had gone wrong? Their leader had had a vision. He was told this was the time; this was the end of time. Sheepishly, one by one, family by family, they slipped away and returned to their homes and the madness they saw in the world. They shrugged and said of their ill-fated brush with eternity, "Perhaps God's time is not our time."

This scene has repeated itself again and again since Jesus' death, resurrection, and ascension. There was the hysteria of the coming of the year 1000 and the anticipation of the coming of the third millennium. A thousand years ago at the close of the first millennium, the signs were present just as they were when the second millennium drew to a close. There were floods, disease, war, and rumors of war. Prophets of doom predicted the end of the world.

William Miller (1782-1849) was an Adventist who erroneously predicted Jesus' second coming. Rev. Miller studied and probed the Old Testament book of Daniel and the Book of Revelation in the New Testament in search of the time when Jesus would return. He concluded that the world as he knew it would end on March 21, 1844. When this day passed without incident, a new prediction was made, October 22, 1844, but this, too, proved to be a day like any other day.

Religious leaders call this eschatology—the end times. It is strange that so many people supposedly look forward to the second coming, but they also fear it. Jesus is supposed to come and judge the world. The dead are resurrected to stand with the living. Some, it is said, are destined to experience the eternal torment of hell, and others will share with Jesus 1000 years of peace. This is a strange theology of a God that is reported to be love itself.[1]

Perhaps there is another answer to why the people on the hill were disappointed by Jesus' failure to return as they anticipated. Their justification was that God's time was not their time. It is probably more true to say that in God there is no time, for God's "clock" marks eternity and perpetually chimes an eternal now. However, at the core, there is another possibility that any spiritual seeker must consider. Perhaps the second coming is not what we think it is or what we have been told it is by our religious leaders. Perhaps we do not understand the second coming because we do not yet fully understand the meaning and purpose of the first coming.

It is vitally important that we do not think of the second coming solely in Christian terms. As we will see in the second section of this book, other religions share the idea of a wayshower or spiritual leader who comes again. Certainly it is appropriate for anyone who wonders about spiritual things to contemplate why Jesus came; however, let us expand our thinking to ask why any of the great spiritual leaders, wayshowers, and masters came to the earth. There have been many. They are so well known that they are usually called by a single name: Buddha, Mohammed, Jesus, Paul, Moses. People who live in lands far from the home and provinces of these spiritual giants still know who they are.

Many Missions Or One?

Moses came to lead his people out of bondage. Nearly every wayshower's mission could be described this way. Initially, Siddhartha Gautama, a prince of Sakya who became the Buddha, was shielded from the ills of the world by his father, the king, but eventually he witnessed the pain and suffering of the people of the world. This was the beginning of Siddhartha's search for meaning that led him to the Bodhi tree where, through enlightenment or wakefulness, he was released from bondage to the world. Our Hindu friends likewise want "liberation (*moksha*) — release from the finitude that restricts us from the limitless being, consciousness, and bliss our hearts desire."[2]

Seemingly, Paul's purpose was to spread the Christian message to the Gentiles, but his central teaching ultimately became *"...it is no longer I who live, but Christ who lives in me"* (Gal. 2:20). Did Jesus come to save the world? This is what we have been taught, but he said he came *"to bear witness to the truth."*[3] And what of Mohammed? What was his purpose? His followers conquered most of the known world, but the heart of Islam is surrender to God. The mystical arm of Islam, Sufism, aspires to a direct experience of the presence of God. Surely, this requires a profound surrender that paradoxically leads to liberty.

Nearly every culture has its wayshower—the one united with God who lives life differently from the rest of us, but who calls us to live as he lives. Some wayshowers began as ordinary men. Saul, who became Paul, crusaded against Jesus and his followers. He held the garments of those who mortally stoned Stephen, the first Christian martyr. However, a spiritual experience on the road to Damascus led to his transformation. Moses, the Hebrew raised in Pharaoh's court, murdered an Egyptian and fled into the wilderness and eventually encountered his God not at the foot of the Bodhi tree, but while standing in awe of a burning bush.

Mohammed's birth in 570 A.D. was tragic, for his father died a few days before he was born and within six years his mother was likewise gone. Like Siddhartha, he was sensitive to human suffering, but his life in the caravan business kept him detached from the anguish of others around him. Mohammed's place of illumination was a cave on Mount Hira where he frequently rested in solitude. On what the Muslims call the Night of Power, he received his commission:

> *Proclaim in the name of your Lord who created!*
> *Created man from a clot of blood.*
> *Proclaim; your Lord is the Most Generous,*
> *Who teaches by the pen;*
> *Teaches man what he knew not.*
>
> (Koran 96:1-3)

Jesus' virgin birth was miraculous, but like so many of the other wayshowers, his mission began after a period of solitude. In Jesus' case, He spent 40 days in the wilderness rather than in a cave or beneath a tree. He faced his temptations just as Siddhartha did and then began his ministry by proclaiming, *"...the kingdom of heaven is at hand"* (Mt. 4:17).

This simplistic look at the lives of some of the world's great wayshowers reveals that they have much in common with each other. If they were to meet on a single day, surely their sense of oneness with the Creator and with their fellow human beings would naturally lead to a loving communion with one another.

Why can't we be like them? They taught many truths that lead us from bondage, but the most remarkable thing is that they lived what they taught. They call us not to teach, but to live; to live in harmony with one another and in oneness with the Creator.

Ghandi, a modern day Moses who helped to free India from British colonial rule, believed in the principle of *ahimsa.* Underlying the powerful driving force of Ghandi's commitment to freedom was the unity of all life and harmlessness. Jesus, likewise, enjoined his followers to turn the other cheek. The *Bhagavad-gita* sounds a similar refrain: *Non-violence means that one should not do anything that will put others into misery or confusion.*[4] Likewise, the Koran speaks of the power of genuine forgiveness. *A kind word with forgiveness is better than almsgiving followed by injury.*[5]

The tragedy is that we are like children who insist that their father is better than another child's father. Our cultural roots run so deep that we fail to see the common ground we share. Instead, we insist that our wayshower is the one who must be followed and our religion's practices are the ones that lead to liberation and oneness with God. It is time to grow up and put away childish things.

There have been many wayshowers. They were seeds cast by the Tree of Life. In each instance, they bore incredible fruit. Millions have followed, not always with understanding, but with a faith that life can be more than it appears to be. I believe that if anyone probes the depth of his religion and strives to answer the question of why his wayshower came, he will discover the purpose of the first coming. And if those who asked why the wayshower came gathered to share their discoveries, they would find that the purpose, the mission, the commission was the same. The words would differ, but the basic message from the Creator to the wayshower would be the same.

You are my appointed one. You will show the people the way to freedom. You will tell them that the path leads through Me. I am the only One and to Me they must come. When they experience Me as you have, then they will be free, and I will have what I have always wanted, a voice through which to share my love and compassion and hands through which to act in loving and compassionate ways.

Notes

1 I John 4:16.

2 Huston Smith, *The World's Religions.* HarperCollins Publishers, 1991. 21.

3 John 18:37.

4 A. C. Bhaktivedanta Swami Prabhupada, *Bhagavad-gita As It Is*, The Bhaktivedanta Book Trust, 1968. 165.

5 Surah II, 263.

Chapter Two

A New Species

Finding What They Found In Us

The wayshowers lived lives unlike our own. Their values were different from ours. For instance, they valued our lives over their own. This is contrary to the self-preservation instinct that we are told is the dominant force of our psyche. Instead, the strongest urge of these spiritual giants was service and the outworking of a divine plan. Their experience of the presence of God, their understanding of the divine blueprint, and their desire to serve humanity charged them with boundless energy enabling them to produce enormous amounts of good works and to accomplish the seemingly impossible.

They accessed divine power through humility, they dealt with their fellow human beings with non-resistance, and they were powerful beyond measure, but there was also a meekness about them. They took no thought for their lives, what they would eat, drink, or wear, but all their needs were met.

In many ways, they appeared different and set apart from the rest of humanity. It was as if they were a different species, and yet they called us to live in the way that they lived and to value the things that they valued. It would be cruel beyond words to cause us to aspire to a life that was beyond our grasp. What they asked us to do, we must be capable of doing.

Perhaps the first thing they asked us to do was to look at ourselves differently. They must have seen something in us that we have not yet seen. We look at ourselves and see flesh and blood. We venture inside ourselves and become aware of thoughts and feelings. Within us there is joy and anguish. There are thoughts that uplift and thoughts that are destructive.

These spiritual giants were not strangers to what moves within us and what it means to be human. They faced their temptations. They could have abused their power, but they did not. They knew their lives could have meaning and that they could make a difference.

When we view anything through the eyes of human consciousness, we see dimly; we see separation. The chasm in behavior between us and the wayshowers is vast, but they told us that we have the potential to do the things that they did. Jesus, Christianity's wayshower, boldly stated, *"...you can do the things that I do"* (Jn 14:12). *"You, therefore, must be perfect, as your heavenly Father is perfect"* (Mt. 5:48). The sacred literature of Buddhism has its own call to follow the wayshower. *Whatever action a great man performs, common men follow. And whatever standards he sets by exemplary acts, all the world pursues.*[1] The Koran reminds the Prophet that he is not the provider, keeper, or controller of anyone. At best, he is a guide and a friend.[2]

Jesus was remarkable as were the Buddha and Mohammed. They did extraordinary things, but the most incredible thing is that they called us to join them. Surely their faith in us was not misplaced. They made a discovery about our potential, and they tried to help us discover it ourselves, but for the most part we have been too busy worshipping them, memorizing what they said, and building religious institutions to find what they found in us.

The Difference

Our innate potential may be identical to that of the spiritual giants who walked the earth, but there is a reason why we are not doing what they called us to do. When I was in ministerial school, oral exams were conducted during my years in training. As a ministerial candidate, I gave a verbal presentation of a spiritually helpful idea and then a group of as many as 15 ordained ministers questioned me on the presentation and a variety of related subjects. I recall one of the questions I was asked. *What is the difference between you and Jesus?* An answer quickly entered my mind—consciousness. My one word reply satisfied the examining minister.

The difference between a typical human being and a wayshower is consciousness. We live in the world, but we live out of, or from, our consciousness. Our values, attitudes, beliefs, thoughts, and feelings give birth to our behavior. However, although we differ in consciousness from the spiritual giants who have gone before us, at the core we are the same. This is blasphemy for many people. Defenders of the faith rise up in protest. They must, and it is important that they do, but it is also important that there are people who are explorers of aspects of our spirituality that are unknown to a majority of the human family. Just as some must protest and defend, others must explore and consider beliefs uncharted by the religious community.

We may not be expressing as the wayshowers did, but we are capable of grand acts of compassion and of sacrificing our lives for others. Ordinary people like you and me can at a moment's notice forget themselves and put themselves at risk to help a stranger.

Many years ago, an aircraft crashed in the icy waters of the Potomac River while taking off from Washington National Airport. A television audience watched the rescue operations. One man jumped into the frigid waters to help a woman who had lost her grip on a helicopter rescue line that was dragging her to safety. Without regard for his own life, the man pulled the woman to safety. He said he did not even feel the cold until he was in an ambulance taking him and the woman to the hospital.

Some survivors clung to the fuselage of the aircraft waiting for a helicopter to bring them a rope ladder to take them to safety. One of the passengers grasped the rope and could have been pulled to safety, but he passed the rope to a fellow survivor who was then rescued. He passed the rope several times. Finally, when the rope was brought for him, the man was gone. He had lost his grip and slid beneath the surface of the water. He had given his life for others. This is our potential. We defy definition and the reported "truth" that self-preservation is our strongest impulse. The truth is that expressing our spiritual nature is our strongest urge.

Whenever such events occur, the spiritual giants who have gone before us must approve, for one of us has risen into a new state of mind and heart. Through forgetfulness, by taking no thought for his or her life, one of us has discovered a wellspring of courage and strength that the wayshowers saw within us.

Sowing Seeds Of The New Species

The human family has been evolving for eons. Anthropologists probe our past and try to piece together our evolution from bone fragments of our prehistoric kinsmen. They want to find the missing link to our most distant ancestors. They seek to build a bridge to the past in order to understand who we are today. Perhaps there is a missing link to our past; however, I believe there are links to our future.

Mohammed, Buddha, and Jesus and such people as Ghandi and Mother Teresa of Calcutta are the links to our future. They showed us what we are capable of doing and being; they showed us our next step in evolution. Our exploration is not of bone fragments or even our DNA. We shall concern ourselves with the engine of evolution—consciousness. This is the catalyst of our growth. It is our evolving consciousness that will allow us to see what we are and why we are here.

The first coming, the birth and life of a wayshower, is the Tree of Life sowing a seed of the new species, the next step in our evolution. When this seed sprouts and grows, an extraordinary life is lived. This person always invites us to join him or her.

This is part of the divine plan. We are created in our Creator's image, so our God can have an avenue of expression. I believe we can sense this. Peace, not conflict, is our natural state. Wars and struggles between individuals have continued for millennia, but we hold to the promise of peace. We will never let it go because we intuitively know it is our destiny. Compassion is our true passion. Thoughts of me and mine may motivate some of our actions, but happiness comes when we are kind. A simple act of compassion will fill us with a joy so great that we can hardly contain it. And our fulfillment comes when we receive something not from outside ourselves, but when a creative expression surges from within. If there is anything that is truly addictive, it is creativity.

Save Us Now

Wayshowers are often called saviors. This is particularly true when it is anticipated that a wayshower will return. The prevailing thought is that they will judge us and do for us what we have not been able to do for ourselves. It is interesting that in religion we persist in holding to this belief. We think this is God's plan, but no mature parent would treat a child this way. Parents do not serve as "saviors" for their children. Part of being a mother or father is helping our offspring discover their inner resources. "Punishment" is more the consequence of the child's action than it is an attempt to inflict pain.

Only by discovering their inner resources and who they are can children become adults who contribute to the unfoldment of the race. Only through the discovery of inner resources can our species evolve and grow.

Salvation comes through this discovery. This is part of the mission of the first coming. The saviors ask us to look within ourselves and discover what the Creator has placed within us. To even begin to explore this inner realm is to begin a new life.

Notes

1 A. C. Bhaktivedanta Swami Prabhupada, *Bhagavad-gita As It Is*, The Bhaktivedanta Book Trust, 1968. 165.
2 Shaykh Fadhlalla Haeri, *A Journey of the Self, A Sufi Guide to Personality*. HarperCollins San Francisco, 1989. 157.

Chapter Three

The Nicodemus Society

Now there was a man of the Pharisees, named Nicodemus, a ruler of the Jews. This man came to Jesus by night and said to him, "Rabbi, we know that you are a teacher come from God; for no one can do these signs that you do, unless God is with him." Jesus answered him, "Truly, truly, I say to you, unless one is born anew, he cannot see the kingdom of God." Nicodemus said to him, "How can a man be born when he is old? Can he enter a second time into his mother's womb and be born?" Jesus answered, "Truly, truly, I say to you, unless one is born of water and the Spirit, he cannot enter the kingdom of God. That which is born of the flesh is flesh, and that which is born of the Spirit is spirit. Do not marvel that I said to you, 'You must be born

anew.' The wind blows where it wills, and you
hear the sound of it, but you do not know
whence it comes or whither it goes; so it is with
everyone who is born of the Spirit."
Nicodemus said to him, "How can this be?"
Jesus answered him, "Are you a teacher of
Israel, and yet you do not understand this?"

(Jn. 3:1-10)

Born Of Spirit

Nicodemus was a learned religious leader of Israel. He was well-versed in the law and his religion's sacrificial practices. He longed for the coming of the messiah and the establishment of the kingdom of God. Like most people of his time, Nicodemus thought of the kingdom of God as an earthly, political kingdom, one without the dominance of Rome.

His fellow Pharisees were concerned about this itinerant rabbi, Jesus of Nazareth, and wanted to be rid of him. Other false christs had risen up in Israel and when the people rallied around them and stood in defiance of Rome, Caesar's legions crushed the rebellion, and Jerusalem was filled with the sounds of mourning. The roads leading to Jerusalem were lined with the crucified followers of another false prophet.

Nicodemus must have seen Jesus differently, for he came secretly to talk with him. The Pharisee was intrigued with the divine power that he saw expressed by this unlearned prophet from Galilee. Jesus must have recognized Nicodemus as a seeker of truth. He did not purport to have all the answers like many of the other religious leaders. Nicodemus, it seemed, hardly knew what questions to ask.

Intuitively Jesus knew that although Nicodemus was a religious leader, he had not yet awakened to the Spirit within him. Jesus also sensed that this is what Nicodemus wanted; this is what he needed—a spiritual awakening. This is critical because unless a person has a spiritual awakening, or is born anew, he cannot see the kingdom of God.

Even though Nicodemus was a spiritual leader, he did not understand personal spiritual awakening. He, like most of the world, believed that the kingdom of God could come on earth without an awakening. The Jewish belief of ancient times was that if all the Jews could abide by the law for a single day, the kingdom would come. Today, Christians believe the kingdom will come when Jesus returns. The Muslims believe that the kingdom will come when the Hidden Imam reveals himself.

Regrettably, we have been a Nicodemus society not understanding the nature of personal spiritual awakening and the role it plays in the transformation of the world. The rebirth that Jesus spoke of to Nicodemus was not entering once more into the womb, but awakening spiritually, and seeing for the first time what the wayshowers had seen.

Today, many religious leaders preach about salvation while little realizing that it is a person's spiritual birth that will save them. Rather than preaching a theology of salvation, it would be better if today's spiritual leaders told the people about spiritual awakening. This is what Jesus did. Time and time again, he described the kingdom of God, and in his conversation with Nicodemus, he stated that only one who is born anew will see the kingdom of God. Nicodemus asked Jesus how it could be that a person enter again into his mother's womb. Jesus asked Nicodemus how it could be that a religious leader, a ruler of the Jews, did not understand the nature of spiritual awakening.

Let us not be too hard on Nicodemus. We have been a Nicodemus society searching for something, but not realizing that it is our own awakening. How often have we wished that we could start over again? Perhaps we even wished that we could be physically born again and not make the mistakes we had made. No one can undo the past, but we can start over again if we are willing to begin anew. A spiritual awakening will not only give us a new start; it will bring into being a new creation that is more attuned to unseen spiritual forces and more willing to live a life of purpose.

For Jesus and the world's wayshowers, the kingdom was not coming. It was here. They looked beyond appearances and saw what we have not been able to see. They saw it because they were spiritually awake. They wanted this same experience for us. Even in the midst of winter, Jesus pointed to the barren fields and proclaimed, *"...the fields are already white for harvest."*[1] This is what it means to have eyes to see and ears to hear.

The Purpose Of The First Coming

The wayshowers, the seeds of the Tree of Life, came to show us our potential and our capabilities. They asked us to see life as they saw it, sacred and beautiful. They never said, "Worship me!" Always in one form or another, they said, "Follow me."

They taught us about spiritual awakening because they knew that we were created not only to be born of water, but also to be born of Spirit. Spiritual awakening is each person's destiny. It is also the destiny of humanity. An awakened individual provides Spirit with an avenue of expression. Whenever even one of us awakens to our spiritual nature, a door opens through which God can do Its work. The truth is no longer a possibility. It is reality. One person who is spiritually awake impacts the world and tends to awaken others from their slumber. Imagine the impact of a race of beings who are avenues for Spirit's expression. This is the power of the third coming.

Notes

1 John 4:35.

Chapter Four

The Cosmic Christ
The Universal Buddha

A Line Becomes A Circle

In 1942 a houseguest staying with Mahatma Gandhi asked him why he, a non-Christian, would have a picture of Jesus on a mud wall of his hut. The Hindu saint replied, "I am a Christian, and a Hindu and a Moslem, and a Jew."[1] Gandhi's reply captured the heart and spirit of the wayshowers that lived centuries and millennia before him. The Creator is not distinctly Christian, Hindu, Buddhist, Muslim, or Jewish. Jesus, for instance, is considered the founder of Christianity, but he was a Jew; and I suspect his love of and oneness with humanity would not permit him to think of himself as a member of one religious sect or another. All great souls and spiritual leaders tap a universal stream of consciousness where all people are brothers and sisters rather than members of a particular religion. They look at people who call themselves Christians, Jews,

Buddhists, Hindus, and Muslims and see human beings—some happy, some sad, some religious, others secular, but everyone is seen as God's creation.

Mahatma Gandhi's statement indicates that he identified with the human family. His race was human, and his religion was oneness. Although he was a Hindu, he was considered by many people to be the most Christ-like person on earth. His spirituality drew a circle that included all of us rather than a line over which he asked us to cross. He probably could have converted many Christians to Hinduism, but instead he remarked, "I do believe that in the other world there are neither Hindus, nor Christians, nor Moslems."2

The Wayshower's Vision

Wayshowers such as Ghandi look beyond religious nomenclature and practices, and therefore they are able to see the spirituality that underlies every religion. For instance, they knew that our true nature is spiritual rather than Christian, Hindu, Buddhist, Jewish, or Moslem. When will Christians finally spy the Christ in Moslems who pray five times a day? When will Moslems see the Hidden Imam in the untouchables, *harijan,* of India? Will the people of the earth understand their own spiritual path so thoroughly that they will see that the Buddha of the Buddhist, the Christ of the Christians, and the Krishna of the Hindus is the same spiritual nature that rests in silent repose in every human being?

Most of humankind believes that Christ was a man named Jesus who was born in a stable in Bethlehem. We think that a prince of Sakya named Siddhartha became the Buddha and that a man currently in hiding is the Hidden

Imam. Wayshowers have a more expanded vision that asks us to look beyond the historical person.

Jesus, Mohammed, Moses, and Buddha and such spiritual giants as Paul, Ghandi, and Mother Teresa of Calcutta discovered God's presence within themselves. They concluded that what they had found in themselves was also present in every human being. This is a profound and far-reaching conclusion that every wayshower has made about his fellow human beings. Paul, for instance, wrote to the Colossians of a *mystery hidden for ages and generations, but now made manifest...Christ in you, the hope of glory.*[3]

This is the cosmic Christ that is within each of us. It is the universal Buddha nature through which we find liberty and happiness. The challenge for us is not simply to acknowledge the presence of God in our wayshowers, but to follow them in making a similar discovery about ourselves. How else can we live the lives that they called us to live?

Let us not deny the historical reality of Jesus, Buddha, Moses, and Mohammed; however let us come to know that there was a principle at work in these spiritual giants that is universal and a part of everyone. It is the essence of every human being. This was their discovery, and we are called to become explorers and make the same breakthrough. The wayshowers of every age pointed the way, but they cannot walk the path for us.

The Perfect One

Nearly every religion has the image of the perfect one. This being has many names: for Christians it is Christ, for Jews the Messiah, the Hindus call him Krishna, the Buddhists call their perfect one Buddha, and the savior of Islam is the Hidden Imam. Just as we have speculated that there is one God and therefore one divine plan, could it be that there is one idea in the mind of God of the perfect being? Let us put aside the popular names used by the religions of the world and consider that the perfect one is the image of God.

There may be one idea in the mind of God of the perfect one, but this single idea has manifested itself in the form of wayshowers such as Jesus, Buddha, St. Francis of Assisi, and saints and holy people of every religion of the world. Surely, there are countless other individuals who have lived godly lives, and yet history has never recorded their names. They lived in obscurity, but they touched the lives of everyone around them.

The perfect one, the image of God, is more than a person. It is the essence of every human being. At our core, we are spiritual. The good news is that the image of God can live as a human being. Through the ages, we have seen this happen. This brings us to a powerful principle active in our lives—the individuality principle.

The Individuality Principle

Let me share a mundane example of this important principle before returning to the idea in the mind of God of the perfect being. All games of sport have rules or principles that outline how the game is played. When a game is played, even a touch football game at a family reunion picnic, the principles underlying the game are individualized, that is, they are expressed. They move from the abstract to the concrete. Each autumn the principles and rules are made manifest at high school football games as well as during January when the Super Bowl game determines the best football team in the world.

A recipe is another example of individuality. A recipe for a chocolate cake cannot be eaten, but when the ingredients outlined in the recipe are properly mixed and baked, the recipe is individualized and comes alive as a chocolate cake—until the very last bite.

Do you remember the geometry class where you learned that a triangle is a three-sided, two dimensional form with three interior angles totaling 180 degrees? All triangles, you were told, had these same characteristics. The sides and angles were a kind of recipe or "rules of the game" through which you could create a triangle. In fact, once you understood the principle behind a triangle there was no limit to the number of triangles you could draw. Every three sided form you made individualized the idea of a triangle.

Individuality is everywhere. Not only does it touch our physical world through the games we play, food we eat, and the geometric forms around us, it also holds the promise of a life of great purpose, creativity, and happiness. The truth is that at the heart of the divine plan is the image of God waiting to be individualized—to come alive and to be made manifest. The image of God is like a seed. Within every acorn there is a great oak tree. No one can see the tree within the seed, but it is there ready to be individualized, ready to come into being.

Each Of Us An Image of God-Seed

Each of us is an image of God-seed destined to sprout and grow and give expression to the nature of our Creator. Defenders of the faith cry out, "No, blasphemy. This cannot be. It is not true." Yes, it is true. In fact, in every age we are called to let the image of God be individualized. During medieval times, a German priest named Meister

Eckhart made the following bold statements.

The seed of God is in us...Now the seed of a pear tree grows into a pear tree, a hazel seed into a hazel tree, the seed of God into God.[4]

God lies in the maternity bed, like a woman who has given birth, in every good soul which has abandoned its self-centeredness and received the indwelling of God.[5]

What help is it to me that the Creator gives birth to the Son unless I too give birth to him? It is for this reason that God gives birth to the divine child in a perfect soul and lies in the maternity bed so that God can give birth to the child again in all his works.[6]

Each statement called the people to let the image of God come into being. Eckhart called for the coming of the Cosmic Christ, for he knew that it was not enough that we were made in God's image and likeness. This image must come alive and be individualized upon this planet.

Meister Eckhart's statements uttered over 600 years ago are revolutionary today. If we think of the Christ as Jesus, we will never understand Meister Eckhart's statements on birth. He thought of each person as a Mary because each of us is charged with the responsibility of allowing the image of God, the Christ, to be born in the manger of our souls. Meister Eckhart was a Christian, so he called the spirit of God within us the Christ. A Buddhist understanding the need for our spiritual birth would undoubtedly call the indwelling Presence our Buddha nature.

The words are not as important as understanding the

process that is destined to occur in our souls. The spirit of God is within us, in everyone of us, and it is part of the divine plan that it be born into the world. This is what Jesus was trying to tell Nicodemus when he came in the night to talk to Jesus. The wayshowers understood that through our own spiritual awakening we experience the presence of God. We are changed forever, and our Creator then has an avenue through which to express Its love, compassion, joy, wisdom, and power.

The Purpose Of The First Coming

The first coming was the birth and life of a wayshower. Each came to help us live. Each also came to help us discover our spiritual nature. A cosmic principle is at work in us. We are a seed cast to the stars. Like a wildflower that grows from a crevice in the wall of a cliff, we, too, feel the urge to live. Nothing can deny this desire because it is more than our own. The Creator's urge is in us. A divine plan is seeking expression. Now is the time for the second coming, but it is not what we think.

We look to our wayshowers to save us, while they are showing us the way to salvation. We believe they are different from us, but they are calling us to do the things that they did. We know they take sustenance from unseen realms. They eat and drink food that we do not know. They see wholeness where we see sickness, plenty where we see famine. We call for them to help us, and they call for us to help Spirit give expression to Its divine plan. We ask that they come again, and they say that they have been with us always. We ask them to return, and they will—when we finally allow the cosmic Christ and the universal Buddha to live in us.

Notes

[1] Louis Fischer, *Gandhi His Life and Message for the World.* Mentor Books, 1954. 130.

[2] *Ibid.,* 131.

[3] Colossians 1:26-27.

[4] Matthew Fox, *Breakthrough: Meister Eckhart's Creation Spirituality in New Translation.* Doubleday & Co., 1980. 118.

[5] *Ibid.,* 93.

[6] *Ibid.*

Section Two

The Second Coming

Chapter Five

God's Rebellion

A Call For Change

There seems to be a perpetual call for change. We need stricter gun laws, campaign contribution reform, moral presidential and legislative leadership, and a way to resolve national, world, and religious conflict without the use of force. Even the neighbors' kids need to change their habit of playing loud music late at night. And there is more. Innate to our souls is the compelling realization that life is change, and that there is always more, always a greater wholeness seeking expression. In most instances, change will take place over years. People working from within the current system will enact reform. Over the course of time, the children next door will alter their late night practices. Even the wholeness that seeks to express itself as our lives will steadily move from the unseen realm of Spirit into the tangible world where we live and move and have our being.

However, there have been times when revolution was

the path to change. The system, the way it has always been, was so entrenched and its roots ran so deep that only a radical departure from status quo could bring about the needed transformation. Even after the system (the tree) was felled, the roots had to be dug up, so their grip on the earth could never be reestablished. Oppression, injustice, and prejudice could no longer be tolerated—not for another moment.

Oppressed people always reach a time when they will no longer endure the pain inflicted upon them by their masters. No longer will they tolerate limitation and inequity, so they rise up. History records the wars, rebellions, and revolutions of liberation. It is clear that although people's liberty can be restricted for generations, eventually the oppressed will secure their freedom through any necessary means. If no one will stand up for them, they will stand up for themselves. If they must rebel, they rebel.

Many religions have a revolutionary element because they teach that the change that will ultimately bring peace on earth will come through radical revolution. Eschatology, from the Greek eschaos which means last, is the study of God's rebellion. No longer will the Presence be held in bondage in our souls. No longer will love be an unrealized ideal. Spirit demands Its expression. Oppression, decadence, and injustice must be replaced by compassion and justice for all.

A student of eschatology learns of God's planned radical dismantling of the world humankind has created. Much of the sacred literature of the planet prophesies that a new world will come through the demise of the current order of things. Apparently, drastic measures are required because the current state of humankind cannot be reformed from within.

Traditional Christianity prophesies that God's rebellion will begin with the second coming of Jesus. The itinerant rabbi of Nazareth will return and judge the world. People will be separated into groups of those who will be punished eternally for their misdeeds and those who are destined to live in serenity and in God's presence. Peace will reign for a thousand years, and then a final judgment will banish evil forever.

I believe the world is destined to be free of wars, famine, and injustice. I believe it will begin with a second coming, but not one that brings Jesus to the earth again. The second coming I have discovered must march across the earth not by consuming one nation after another, but by touching one human heart and then another and then another. This, as we will see, is the second coming that Jesus taught, and which is the spiritual foundation of the second coming idea that is a part of many religions of the earth.

The Second Coming Motif

The idea of the second coming is not solely a Christian belief. Although the second coming motif is not present in all religions, many spiritual paths include a savior. For instance, the Shi'ite Moslems believe that the Hidden Imam will emerge from hiding and "he will fill the earth with justice just as it is now full of iniquity."[1] Chinese Buddhism of the 4th century anticipated the return of Maitreya who would bring an utopian kingdom to earth. The Hopi Indians believe that a Christ-like being named Pahana will save the world. The Babylonians had their eschatological savior named Saoshyant. Even some editions of the King Arthur tales say that Arthur will return and begin a reign of justice and peace.

The second coming motif contains two themes. The first is salvation. It is foretold that a savior or deliverer will come to save the people and the world from the influence of evil. As we will see, messianic movements are prevalent on the earth today. Wherever there is oppression, the subjugated people call for a savior and the end of the world as they are currently experiencing it. Their oppressors are so strong that only a savior sent from God can overcome those who dominate them. The second theme is the return. The savior has either disappeared and is prophesied to return or has died and will return as a sign that God's kingdom is emerging from the ashes of the world that used to be.

The roots of these beliefs are not Christian. In fact, they run deeper than any religion or culture. Innate to us is the hope of salvation and a better world. Whenever we are in pain, we long to be free of our anguish. Throughout the ages, people in distress have sought a savior, someone to deliver them from their bondage and pain. The cry has gone out, "Help us," and from within the greater soul of humankind, an answer is heard. "There is one who will deliver you."

And so we look for the deliverer. Great men and women have come. They have helped thousands, millions of us. Mother Teresa of Calcutta helped tens of thousands of untouchables and in the process touched the hearts of people around the world. Ghandi helped to free a nation. There are thousands of unheralded individuals in every country giving themselves unselfishly for the common good. We will never know the names of most of them, but they are love in action. However, even the spiritual giants who were clearly God's emissaries did not save humanity. A casual look at the world today shows that it is still in need of salvation. Apparently, the savior has not yet come, or he must return to finish what he began.

The Return

The return or the coming again is a belief deeply embedded in our psyche. Our distant kinsmen observed numerous cycles in nature. Every day the sun seemed to die at dusk and return or be reborn at dawn. The lunar cycle repeated itself every 29.5 days as the moon moved through its phases and traversed the night sky. Over the course of a year, keen observers could witness the solar cycle as the sun moved through its solstices and equinoxes. The stars marched in an orderly fashion through the heavens. The three stars in the constellation Orion could easily be seen in the northern hemisphere and were expected to return at the same time each year.

Everywhere our ancestors looked, they saw the cycles of life. In most areas of the world, nature's renewal was evident. As early humans ceased their nomadic life and began to till the earth, they became increasingly aware of the position of the sun that marked the coming of the growing season and the fertility cycles that governed the growth of crops. First, there was the seed, apparently lifeless, yet filled with the gift of life. From the seed came the blade of grass, then the ear, and finally the grain that could be pounded into flour and baked to sustain the family.

This was more than a cycle of seed to grain to bread; life depended upon the harvest. It was a cycle of life. How natural it was for this mysterious cycle to become a part of the spiritual life of the people. Agricultural communities were established near the basins of the Nile, Tigris and Euphrates, and Ganges rivers. These rivers consistently flooded their banks and replenished the soil that sustained the life of the inhabitants.

Early in our existence, the return was impressed upon our psyche and naturally became a part of our worship practices and religious beliefs. Even death was ultimately viewed as a birth, a return to life, as evidenced by the remains of kinsmen who were placed in the fetal position in graves over 50,000 years ago. Just as seeds emerged from the darkness of the earth and were born again, so were we destined to experience a rebirth in the next life. Joseph Campbell, the noted mythologist, stated in a video on the mystery religions of ancient Greece that resurrection or coming back to life again was a belief prevalent in myths around the world.

A Brief History Of The Second Coming

The seed of the second coming or the return was sown in the minds of our ancestors as they witnessed the cycles of nature around them. Religious beliefs did not come from sacred scripture or even the oral traditions of our distant relatives. They came from our souls and then found their way into our beliefs and eventually into our holy writ. First ideas grow in our collective consciousness, and then they find form in our beliefs, rituals, values, and culture.

The great Egyptian myth of Osiris is believed to be an expression of the flooding of the Nile River.[2] The phenomenon of the mighty river overflowing its banks was considered a sacred event because of its life sustaining properties and therefore worthy of a portrayal of the death and resurrection of a king. According to legend, Osiris was a god-king who was killed and dismembered by his brother, Seth. Isis, Osiris' wife, went on a quest to find the 14 pieces of her husband's body and vowed to put them together again. Incredibly, she was able to reassemble his body and even to become pregnant by him, but she was unable to truly bring him back to earthly life, so he was buried. When Horus, the son of the miraculous pregnancy, came of age, he sought to avenge his father's death. Eventually, he succeeded and killed Seth in a great battle. Horus then found his father in the land of the dead and revived him. Horus was crowned the new king of Egypt, and Osiris became the "ruler of the underworld, symbolic of resurrection and fertility."[3]

The legend illustrates the impact of a natural event on the psyche of a people, and how such an event strides side by side with politics, family strife, the cycle of the growing season, and our desire for justice and an explanation of the mysteries of life and death. Amazingly, there is a consistent theme in the beliefs of people who ceased the nomadic life and settled in communities where crops became the chief source of food. The issue of fertility naturally dominated the religious life of agricultural societies beginning about 9000 B.C. Just as the land and its crops lived, bore fruit and died, so too did the god of fertility live, die, and live again. The people believed that they owed their lives to the god who died and was resurrected again.

The Babylonian god Tammuz was worshipped as a god of fertility and vegetation. The people saw his life and death as an expression of the germination, fruitfulness, and fading away of plant life. In fact, a drama was enacted in which lamentations were performed that mourned Tammuz's death, and a celebration took place when he returned from the dead. Imagine the joy the people felt when they first spied the tender shoots of the vegetation that declared that Tammuz lived and that the people would live another season as well.

The history of the second coming is ancient. It began when primitive humans observed nature's cycles. The idea of the return was firmly planted in our psyche. The roots reached deeper into our souls as many of the nature cycles were wed with daily life and our existence and survival. Beliefs grew up around the fertility cycle, and gods were conceived to help our distant relatives explain the mystery of the birth and resurrection of the crops that sustained them. The next step in the evolution of our consciousness was the belief that an earthly king could die and be born again. Many researchers believe that the idea of human resurrection or return from the dead first appeared in Zoroastrianism in Babylon.[4]

The Future Hope

In a few brief pages, we have trod through the landscape of human consciousness and through thousands of years of evolutionary thought. Admittedly, this is a simplistic view of the progression of belief that will eventually manifest itself as the traditional view of the second coming. However, it is important to understand that our religious and spiritual concepts do not originate in sacred writings. They have their origin in our search for meaning and our sense of something greater than ourselves. From our experience and spiritual yearning came the sacred works of our world.

The future hope of the ancient world was that God would rule. Billions of people today share this same desire. In fact, they believe that God must rule before there will be peace, justice, and compassion on earth. To this end, there has been an evolution of thought. First, there was the idea of a God-appointed king who would rule justly. Likewise there was the idea of a line of kings who would dispense God's justice. This was seen in the Davidic line of kings in Judaism. From the lineage of King David was to come a future hope, a miraculous child who would be a different kind of king. He would not be a charismatic warrior or political figure, but a suffering servant—one who was willing to die for the people.

History records a Canaanite epic poem about a legendary, mythical king named Karit. His title was Servant of El, the supreme god. This servant dies and rises again. Some scholars believe that the Hebrews borrowed this idea from their neighbors and incorporated it into their religious belief system, but it is more likely that this idea of the suffering servant is an idea that began to rise in human consciousness in the minds of many people. If the gods of fertility were willing to die for the people, could an earthly king also be willing to make the same sacrifice?

This is the way ideas evolve in human consciousness. They incubate in us, and then emerge simultaneously around the world at nearly the same time. We know this to be a normal occurrence in scientific thought; why couldn't it be the norm in our spiritual growth as well?

These primitive beliefs laid the foundation of the messiah who would come to establish a divine rule upon the earth. We first saw the cycle of the return in the movement of the heavenly bodies. It is as if we plucked the idea of the return from high above and made it a part of our souls. As we will discover in the chapters to come, it is closer than we think.

Notes

[1] Have Lazarus-Yafeh. *Some Religious Aspects of Islam*. E.J. Brill, Leiden, The Netherlands, 1981. 48-49.

[2] James R. Lewis. *Encyclopedia of Afterlife Beliefs and Phenomena*. Gale Research Inc., 1994. 122.

[3] *Ibid.*, 122.

[4] *Ibid.*, 306.

Chapter Six

The Many Messiahs

The Anointed One

The word messiah from the Hebrew *mashiah* means anointed one. Although the word has come to mean the expected deliverer,[1] its origin lies in the ceremonies used to enthrone kings. For instance, Saul, Israel's first king, was anointed with oil, and so were David and his son Solomon. Oil was a symbol of light, for it was burned to illumine Hebrew homes. To anoint the king with oil was to bless him with light in the hope that the monarch would be an illumined ruler. However, messianic hopes and movements have consistently centered on the ability of the messiah to save people from oppression.

In southern Brazil, Joao Maria, the "saint" founder of the Contestdo movement went from village to village teaching his "true" Christianity. In 1908, he disappeared. His followers refused to believe he died because in many of his sermons he said he would retire to the summit of a mountain until the hour and day when he would return to the people again. Today, nearly a century after his disappearance, many of the people of rural Brazil confidently await his return. Jamaica also has its messiah, Alexander Bedward. The followers of Bedwardism considered him a prophet who would be taken to heaven like Elijah and then return to choose those who deserved heaven's reward. In 1863, Sio-vili, a local Samoan minister of a pagan Christian cult, prophesied the end of the world and the coming of Sisu Alaisa, a native adaptation of name Jesus Christ.[2]

In the twentieth century, Japan experienced the birth of several new religions. They espoused a belief in a living *kami* who could provide healing and personal, earthly blessings. Consistent with messiah movements was the additional belief that the kami would save humanity. The roots of this religion began in 1802 with a woman, Ryuzen Nyorai, whose beliefs were similar to Christianity's—one *kami* who would save the world. The first of these new systems of belief was Kurozumikyo that was founded in 1814. Likewise the native Americans of the Hopi tribe believe in the coming of a savior. He is Pahana, the lost White Brother, who will come after nine signs have been fulfilled.[3] This prophecy was shared by White Feather, an elder of the ancient Bear Clan. According to him, the nine signs have occurred, and therefore the return of Pahana is imminent.

These are lesser known examples of messianic hopes and movements, but they share common beliefs with the future hope of many of the major religions of the world. First, there is a need for change. The greater the need for reform, the greater the sense of expediency and expectation. A savior is coming who calls the people to return to God and to hold in high esteem a spiritual life. This is the prelude to the transformation of the secular society.

Saoshyant, Maitreya, And Mohammad al-Mahdi

Long before Jesus lived, the Persians anticipated the coming of Saoshyant, the savior. This is the classic second coming motif in which Ahuramazda, the god of light, raises up Zarathustra, the founder of Zorasterianism, to wage a final war against the forces of darkness.

Mahayana Buddhism that flourished in the 4th through the 6th century B.C. foretold the coming of Maitreya. This Christ-like savior will appear during a time when evil dominates the world. Justice will finally be established. Buddhists who followed the Mahayana way hoped to be reborn in either Tusita, the celestial realm, or in the worldly paradise of Ketumati.

Shi'ite Muslims await the coming of Mohammed al-Mahdi, "The Guided One." He is the twelfth Imam, Muhammed ibnul Hassan, son of Imam Hasan al-Askari, the 11th Holy Imam. According to Shi'ite Islamic belief, the twelfth Imam was born in 868 A.D. and has been in hiding since he was seven years old. God has kept him alive since the day he went into hiding initially in a cave below a mosque in Samarra in 874 A.D.

For a Shi'ite Muslim the tragedy of Mohammed al-Mahdi's disappearance is that the Imam is the light of the world, but he is not in communication with the world. This is called the Greater Occultation. Muslims long for him to appear (*zuhur*) to humanity, for the Return (*Raj'a*) will signal the coming of the final judgment and final apocalyptic battle with the forces of evil. After the defeat of evil, the Mahdi will rule the world for several years under a perfect government and bring about a perfect spirituality among the peoples of the world.[4] Then Jesus will return.

This theology was at the core of the Islamic Iranian Revolution that brought Ayatullah Ruhollah Khumayni to power. Many believed he was the Hidden Imam and that his return would restore justice to humanity.

More Than History

As I researched the idea of the second coming, I saw that the messianic hope transcends Christianity or any specific religion. It is an idea that is a part of our collective consciousness. Because this is true, we have the capacity to recognize the essence of the second coming motif wherever it appears—in the flooding of the Nile and the story of Osiris or in a Canaanite myth of their fertility god. Greater yet is our ability to recognize the savior/return motif not so much as history or the property of a religion, but as an important part of the spiritual evolution of the human family.

This is the territory we must now explore. In this way, we venture into not only the future of the human species, but also our future as a race of spiritual beings. We can hold to the belief that a savior is coming to save us: a Jewish messiah, a Christian Jesus, a Buddhist Maitreya, a Moslem Imam or even the reborn founder of Zorasterianism. We have waited for these saviors a long time. Perhaps we must be patient and continue to wait, for no one knows when one or all of them will return, or we can explore another possibility. The new approach does not necessarily negate the return of a messiah figure, but it may hasten the deliverance that humanity seeks. We may find that our savior has been waiting for us to realize that each of us has been anointed with oil and that there is a light within us that will guide us to the life our Creator has ordained for us.

Notes

1 Edwin B. Williams. *The Scribner-Bantam English Dictionary*, Bantam Books, 1979. 568.
2 Vittorio Lanternari. *The Religions of the Oppressed*, The New American Library, 1963. 198.
3 Bob Frissell. *Something In This Book Is True*, Frog, Ltd 1997. 32.
4 Richard Hooker. World Culture Home Page, www.seu.edu/~dee/SHIA/HIDDEN.HTM 1997.

Chapter Seven

Your Lord Is Coming

The Year 1000

As the year 1000 approached, many people in Europe were convinced that the end was near. Few people were free, therefore the masses yearned for a savior. Halley's comet dominated the sky and the minds of the faithful when it suddenly appeared in the heavens in 989 A.D. Many people saw it as more than a comet; it was a portent of the coming apocalypse. Monasteries were under attack from the Norsemen raiders. The monks and priests of these sanctuaries of civilization and spirituality were being slaughtered. Christians believed Vikings were instruments of the anti-Christ. They were one more sign that the end was near.

This is the way it is. The events of the current day are interpreted by minds deeply influenced by religious beliefs. It happened as the year 1000 drew near in Europe and repeated itself during the Iranian Islamic revolution as many

Muslims believed they were ushering in a world of justice by casting out the "Great Satan" and installing Ayatollah Khomeini as the supreme leader of Iran.

As the year 1000 dawned, there was no Jesus, so another prediction was made. Perhaps he was coming 1000 years after his death rather than his birth. Disappointment turned to expectation as some of the people eagerly awaited the year 1033, but, of course, Jesus did not appear on the accepted one thousandth anniversary of his death.

Many people hoped that the year 2000 would be the beginning of God's radical revolution. The Hale-Bopp comet appeared in 1997, and some people believed this cosmic traveler was a sign that soon Jesus would return. Like a thousand years before, predictions were made, but like those made one thousand years before, they were in error.

Is this cycle of expectation and disappointment to be repeated every 1000 years or whenever a religious leader thinks he knows the hour of Jesus' return? Ten thousand years from now will we still be waiting? It may be that we are not able to comprehend God's time, but there is also another possibility. Perhaps we have failed to understand the meaning and scope of the second coming or the return motif that is so prevalent in many religions and spiritual movements.

Lo, I Am With You Always

What if the second coming is not a literal return? What if the return motif touches the deepest core of our spiritual lives? What if the second coming is not a world-wide event that the media can cover, but an individual experience that is even now spreading across the earth one person at a time?

It is strange that Christians look for Jesus' return when he said, *"...lo, I am with you always, to the close of the age"* (Mt. 28:20). It seems that the Master was telling us that he never left, that he remains with us always.

I believe three powerful ideas are destined to be joined together, so they make the second coming relevant to daily life. No longer will the return be relegated to prophecy and religious expectancy; instead the return idea will become an integral part of our spiritual lives.

I believe that whenever someone lives according to the life and teachings of the savior of his or her spiritual path, the savior has come again. When a Muslim surrenders to Allah's will, the Hidden Imam has returned. When a Buddhist lives the eightfold path, Maitreya dwells among us. When a Christian turns the other cheek, Jesus has returned. When a Jew realizes that the law is written on his heart, the long awaited messiah has made his entrance.

In Christianity, Paul was the first person in recorded history to experience this return. It grew so powerfully and transformed his life so thoroughly that he said, *"...it is no longer I who live, but Christ who lives in me"* (Gal. 2:20). It was Paul who made the incredible discovery of the indwelling Christ. He wrote in a letter to the Colossians of a mystery hidden for ages and generations, *"...Christ in you, the hope of glory"* (Col.1:27). In this letter, Paul cannot be referring to the itinerant rabbi of Nazareth because Jesus had departed the earth approximately 30 years before the letter was written rather than the ages and generations that Paul references. Paul discovered not Jesus in him, but the spirit of God that makes Its home in every human being. This indwelling spirit is not Jewish or Christian or Muslim or Buddhist. This presence within us is our spiritual essence and nature.

The Second Coming Is Everywhere

The second coming is everywhere. We have looked for portents in the heavens and signs on earth. We have searched the sacred writ of the world's religions. We have watched the clock and the march of time and failed to see the return in every act of compassion and in every feat of forgiveness. Whenever someone gives his life for another, the Christ has returned. On the battlefield, soldiers have taken no thought for their lives. Rescue workers have forgotten themselves in order to try to save those in harm's way. The love in our hearts is activated even when we strive to coax to deep waters a disoriented whale that has wandered into the shallows of a coastal river. Whenever anyone acts upon the conviction of his or her highest values and spiritual beliefs, the spirit of the Master has returned.

Let us not miss the return. It has happened tens of thousands of times since Buddha, Moses, Jesus, and Mohammed walked the earth. Even as the words of this book are read, someone is expressing the love, compassion, and faith of the wayshowers. And the good news is that the coming of the spirit of God occurs more than one or twice; it happens again and again until each of us knows our spiritual nature and the power of God.

Jesus' Return

Jesus has come many times during the last 2000 years. Individuals have experienced the wonder of his consciousness. They have had dreams, seen visions, and heard voices. Francis Bernadone, before he became the saint of Assisi, heard a voice that directed him to rebuild a church. The experience changed Francis' life. People have seen crucifixes come to life and statues of Jesus weep. I, too, have experienced his presence. It happened long ago and totally transformed my life. It opened my soul. I describe it to you now in the hope that it will help you realize that Jesus has come to many people since his seeming departure two millennia ago.

While I was in seminary, a class assignment was given in which members of the class were selected for a panel. Our task was to research what Charles Fillmore, co-founder of the Unity movement, believed about Jesus. In addition to reporting on the Fillmorian understanding of Jesus, each member of the panel was to share his or her personal beliefs about the Master. The night before the assignment was due I returned home from work. Nancy, my wife, and I talked about the assignment that was due the next day. I said to her, "I wish Jesus would come to me and tell me what he is all about."

As soon as I said the words, I felt a presence. Nancy could tell that something was happening. I went into the living room of our mobile home, and Nancy retired to the bedroom to read as she often did. I sat in meditation and waited. To this day, I am not sure how long I sat and experienced the presence of Jesus, but I can tell you that I had a vision of Jesus standing on a mountaintop. He was looking down the slope and speaking to all of humanity. "You can do the things that I do..."[1]

And then he looked to distant summits beyond where he was standing and returned his gaze to the human family and said, "and greater works than these shall you do."[2] In my prayer state, I understood the vision to be a message to me and to humanity. Our destiny is to one day stand in consciousness where Jesus stood. However, he is a wayshower and since the spiritual journey is an infinite one, there is more for Jesus to discover as he continues to explore and push back the limitations that we have imposed upon ourselves.

I never forgot the experience. It was a great grace that touched the depth of my soul. It is also interesting that the next morning before I related the experience to Nancy, she told me that she kept having a series of words move through her mind as she read her novel. She said she thought they were scripture. (At this point, Nancy was not as well versed in the Bible as she is today.) I asked her what words had filled her mind. She answered, "You can do the things that I do and greater things than these shall you do." Nancy had not experienced the vision, but Jesus' consciousness was so strong in the mobile home that the verse had repeated itself again and again.

Often people do not talk about personal experiences such as the one above, but they are happening more than we know. In different cultures, the messenger may be another wayshower, but I believe the experiences are occurring. The return is not delayed; it is happening to people like you and me.

Your Lord Is Coming

We have been told that God's rebellion is through revolution and the overthrow of the forces of evil. No longer will the presence of love that indwells us be contained. No longer will Spirit endure a world of injustice. The end times are coming, we are told, and God's reign of peace will be established as a wayshower comes again. The battle against evil will be won, we will be judged, and a thousand years of peace will begin that will conclude with the final defeat of evil.

I believe God's reign of justice and peace are at hand, but it is not coming through a worldly rebellion. It is coming through revelation and the inner rebellion that naturally comes when we are caught between an old way of thinking and a new way of being. Our world is shaken, and it feels as though we are in an earthquake.[3] We believe things are falling apart when they are actually falling together. The sun and the moon cease to shine.[4] In other words, those things that seemed most stable in our lives as symbolized by the heavenly bodies are no longer so stable. Our relationships have changed because we have changed. The job that provided us with a good income and meaning now seems fruitless and aimless.

This is the beginning of the second coming. It is radical in that there is no upward glance to the heavens. Instead, one more person is awakening to his or her spiritual identity. God is becoming real to this person. Once the individual's faith was based on belief in theological concepts. Now it is rooted in experience. This is the return. Slowly, steadily, people are awakening to their spiritual identity. It is evident in our society that more and more attention is being given to spirituality. It is not because times are hard; it is because it is hard to live when we are not aware of who and what we really are. The typical belief is that the second coming or return will happen to the world. It will, but its pathway is through each individual soul.

People will say that I am a false prophet. This is not true, but there are false prophets.[5] They are not people. They are those things that promise us security, love, and meaning, but they cannot deliver. When we think we are safe and secure because of our job or because of our stock portfolio, we have listened to a false prophet. When a relationship with another person promises us love, we have attached ourselves to a false christ. Security and love are not found in the world. They are gifts that are ours not because of good investments or an ideal mate, but because we have willingly received the gift of God's presence that resides in our souls.

In Matthew 25, Jesus responded to his disciples' query about his return. He speaks of false prophets, wars, and earthquakes. He says these are signs of his coming. This is true because he comes in every age, and people are always waking up to their spiritual identity. It is also true that wars, rumors of war, and earthquakes have always been a part of every society. If you want outer signs, they are always there. However, Jesus points his disciples to a deeper understanding of the second coming. He tells them not to look in the wilderness or in the inner rooms.[6] If there is to be a literal return, it must occur either inside a building of some kind or outside such as an appearance in the clouds. However, he is saying not to look for him in either place. This is because the second coming is the revelation of God to each individual. Look for this to happen in our souls.

It is revealing that in Mt. 24:42, Jesus says to be aware that *your Lord is coming.* This is a powerful statement indicating the personal nature of the second coming. Time and time again throughout the ages, people have experienced the coming of their Christ or Buddha nature. This does not always happen to the learned and the religious. Starr Daily is a good example of a person who awakened spiritually and who touched the lives of many.

Mr. Daily's criminal career began when he was twelve years old. Because he was admittedly poorly skilled at his chosen profession, he spent many years in prison. During one of his imprisonments, he had a dream that changed his life.

> *And then one day there occurred in my dream the man whom I'd been trying to hate for years, Jesus the Christ. He appeared in a garden in every way similar to the one I had seen him in as a child. His physical appearance was also similar. The whole picture had that quiet clarity about it that draws out thematic details of expression, of feeling, of thought, of purpose. He came towards me, his lips moving as though in prayer. He stopped near me eventually and stood looking down. I had never seen such love in a human eye; I had never felt so utterly enveloped in love. I seemed to know consciously that I had seen and felt something that would influence my life throughout all eternity.*
>
> *Presently, He began slowly to fade in the manner of some casual process of dematerialization. Out of what had been a vision of him there emerged a vision of the word Love in large gossamer irregular letters, which remained a moment, and then as he had done, slowly vanished.*[7]

Although serving a life sentence, Starr Daily was eventually released from prison and lived an exemplary life that served as an example of what love can do. In one of his books, *Love Can Open Prison Doors*, he writes of another realization of love he experienced while in solitary confinement.

There in a moment's time the folly of crime and the stupidity of hatred appeared clear-cut in my consciousness, and I got an authentic glimpse of the greatest power in all the world, the power of love, which, when lived with any measure of proficiency, could see you through any emergency, dissolve your toughest problems, cause you to live serenely, triumphantly, and successfully at any time and in any place; that with love on your side as a philosophy of life every obstacle and opposition could be discerned in its true light, as an opportunity to call forth your power.[8]

He elaborates by writing that love is a part of every human being.

I am telling you about a power that resides in the hearts of men, which is a power greater than any power ever to be discovered in the realm of natural science. It is a power possessed by all, but recognized by few.[9]

Starr Daily is a marvelous example of the second coming. Not only was he visited by Jesus in a dream, but Daily began to adopt a loving way of life. The Christ within him came alive and poured itself through him in a way that not only touched the lives of fellow prisoners, but through his writing he touched the lives of the "free" who were imprisoned by their own minds.

The Next Step

There are those who will say that what I have written is nonsense. But what if it is true? What will we do? And what if the traditional view of the return is accurate? What will we do? Do we sit and wait as we have for a thousand years? I say, what would be better than to give ourselves to God, or as a Muslim would say surrender to God, while we wait for the return? And for whom do we await? Is it for the nameless messiah of the Jews or Mohammed Ibnul Hassan of the Muslims or Saoshyant of the few remaining Zoroastrians on earth, Jesus of Christianity, or Maitreya of 4th century B.C. Buddhism? Or could it be that these great ones are waiting for us—waiting for us to awaken to our spiritual nature.

I call for the second coming now. It is time for the human family to awaken. I believe that we are not looking for an end of the world theology; instead we want to discover who we are. In subtle ways we want help in awakening to our spiritual nature. (Spiritual awakening is the theme of the next section of this book.) This call for the return may be radical and revolutionary, but the revolution I believe is coming is revelation. What happened to the wayshowers must happen to us. We must see the burning bush; we must come to realize that everything is ablaze with the presence of God. We must sit under our own Bodhi tree or enter our own cave on a night of power.

Jesus said he would build his church upon revelation. One day, he and his disciples gathered at Caesarea Philippi where an underground river rushed from beneath the earth. It is one of the sources of the River Jordan. Most likely, in the shade of nearby trees, Jesus asked his famous questions.

Now when Jesus came into the district of Caesarea Philippi, he asked his disciples, "Who do men say that the Son of man is?" And they said, "Some say John the Baptist, others say Elijah, and others Jeremiah or one of

*the prophets." He said to them, "But who do you say
that I am"? Simon Peter replied, "You are the Christ,
the Son of the living God." And Jesus answered him,
"Blessed are you Simon Bar-Jona! For flesh and blood
has not revealed this to you, but my Father who is in
heaven. And I tell you, you are Peter, and on this rock
I will build my church..."*

(Matthew 16:13-18)

This is an example of the power of revelation. Jesus saw
that Simon Peter had awakened spiritually. Jesus acknowl-
edged this grand event by saying that flesh and blood had
not revealed the truth to him and by changing his name to
Peter. This was often done in biblical days to indicate that a
person had changed. Peter experienced God's presence. He
spoke the words, *"You are the Christ, the son of the living
God,"* but they were also a revelation to him. This is the
nature of spiritual awakening and the power of revelation.
It moves us, it shocks us. It is upon us in an instant. Revelation is the foundation of every religious movement, or as
Jesus said in this event, the rock upon which the church is
to be built.

The pattern is evident; someone has an experience of
the presence of God. This happened to Buddha, to Moses,
and to Mohammed. The beginning of every religion is the
same—a revelation, an experience of God's presence.
Religions are often born when people have a revelation;
however, this is also the process through which individual
lives are transformed. I have seen this hundreds of times. I
have experienced it. In fact, whenever a person's life is
spiritualized, it is because of an encounter with Spirit.

Revelation is needed. It is more than needed; it is our

destiny. Revelation is the salvation of the world, and each of us has a responsibility to open ourselves to the Creator because when we are spiritually aware, when the heart and spirit of the second coming has occurred, the world will be transformed. This is the third coming that will be addressed in the final section of this book. It is our future hope. The image of God, the prototype being that Spirit created, will draw breath for the first time in every human breast, and the world will never be the same.

Notes

1 John 14:12.
2 *Ibid.*
3 Matthew 24:7.
4 Matthew 24:29.
5 Matthew 24:11,24.
6 Matthew 24:26.
7 Starr Daily. *Love Can Open Prison Doors.* Arthus James Limited, 1947. 36.
8 *Ibid.*, 11.
9 *Ibid.*, 14-15.

Section Three

Spiritual Awakening

Chapter Eight

What The World Needs Now

Breathing Again For The First Time

Most religions tend to focus on converting people to their sect, on saving the sinners, and the future life. Let us give our attention to spirituality rather than religion, the present moment rather than the future, and spiritual awakening instead of saving the sinner from his sin. Much of humanity has had its fill of the stated goals of religion. It is not that the goals are not noble, but that people are yearning for more. In most instances, the seekers don't know what they are looking for, but they know it is more than a particular sect's world or heavenly view. There are pressing issues today. The present life must be more than preparation for life after death. Humanity strives because it instinctively knows that the fulfillment of its spiritual desire is close at hand. Now is the time to go beyond the typical tenets of a particular religion. Now is the time to know and comprehend that which is the mystical foundation of every religion and the destiny of every human being—spiritual awakening.

The good news is that spiritual awakening is occurring.

The work of the wayshowers is being done. The seeds they planted are spouting, growing, and bearing fruit. People all over the world are being roused from their slumber. The second coming is underway. However, let us not think that the awakening depends upon us. True, there are things for us to do and attitudes to adopt, but God is the author of this work. From the beginning, it has always been part of the divine plan that humankind become spiritually awake.

We have human tendencies that deny our spiritual nature, but we also have spiritual tendencies that lead us to a discovery of our true nature and our oneness with God. These tendencies are the subject of "Section Three" of *The Third Coming.* This part of the book outlines the path that lies before us, a path that is our destiny. I believe that the most important and far-reaching experience that a human being can have is spiritual awakening. This is why the wayshowers came. The religions that grew from the seeds they sowed were conceived so we might awaken.

And so we begin the exploration of the most meaningful experience we can have. It changes everything. It is as though we draw breath for the first time. We will look back and see the value of our past experiences, but we will also know that life began when we became aware that the Creator had made Its home in us. This is the heart of the second coming.

Sensing Our Spirituality

It is interesting that the American culture, a culture birthed by a nation created "under God," continues to endorse a futuristic relationship with the Creator while those who first inhabited this land, the Native Americans, believed that a meaningful life required an awareness of the

Great Spirit in the present moment and as a daily p
their lives. This is indigenous spirituality—relevant
practical. The afterlife is respected, but the moment
cherished because it can be filled with a consciousness
Presence.

Judeo-Christian theology may look to another day, but I
venture to say that even those who teach this doctrine yearn
for a relationship with the Creator that touches every part of
their lives. The Native American children became part of
the adult community because they endured the anxiety and
awe of a vision quest. Currently, our society has no rite of
passage that brings our youth into the adult community by
stressing the importance of a relationship with God. Instead, we issue a driver's license. Our theology diminishes a
relevant, daily relationship because it promises communion
with the Creator at a later time. We have been taught to
look to tomorrow while the Great Spirit of every religion
and the Native Americans calls to us today. Seemingly it
has been to the profit of religion to have the people look to
tomorrow and the life hereafter, but I say it is time for
religion to reveal again the message of the wayshowers—
that each human being is made so that he or she can know,
experience, and give expression to the living presence of
God.

This is what the second coming does. It asks us to open
ourselves to an experience of God today. This is the pin-
nacle of the path of awareness for which our species strives.
First, we achieve consciousness. The realization comes—I
am. Naturally we see ourselves in relationship with our
world, with the sun, the mountains, the animals like the
buffalo that sustained those who lived on the prairies, or the
river that overflowed its banks each year and fertilized the

land. Fear of nature as well as awe deepened our connection with the world around us. Next, we turned inward and became aware of our mental and emotional selves. We were astonished by the power of our feelings as well as the impact of the lofty and base thoughts we could hold in mind. Finally, we began to sense our spirituality. We discovered an interior world of thought and feeling, but there was more. There was mystery in us, power, compassion, and love that seemed to transcend flesh and blood.

So first there is the being of flesh who seeks to survive and to continue through its progeny. This person knows the body and the world of form. The mental being accesses ideas and thoughts and eventually discovers that there is a fundamental relationship between attitudes and beliefs and quality of life. The feeling being knows passion and com-passion, anger and fear, forgiveness and love, peace and unrest. This being is body and soul because it sees itself as part of its surroundings and is aware of an inner world that in many ways is more powerful than the forces of nature of the earth. The wind may blow, but it is the thoughts and feelings of the inner person that generate the fear and doubt. It is also the inner realm from which unparalleled strength and courage rise. Often by facing the challenges of life and persisting, we sense our spiritual self. When this occurs, one of the seeds cast by a wayshower has sprouted. From this moment on, we can never be the same. This is the beginning of spiritual awakening and the new life it is destined to bring to us and to the world.

What The World Needs Now

The world needs individuals who are spiritually awake. They know we are more than body, thought, and feeling.

These are the individuals who are taking us into a new millennium. They access ideas seemingly unavailable to other people. They have great powers of persistence. Their strongest urge is not their personal needs or survival, but compassion and love of others. They are humble, non-resistant, and meek, but amazingly powerful. They lead by example. Their decision making is intuitive. They take no thought for their lives, but instead allow their lives to unfold from a divine center. Their values are few, simple, and pure. They are driven by a mission that has been given to them by the Creator. They are interested in the whole rather than their single self. They know true power.

People who are awake are child-like. Awe and wonder are their companions. Mystery is not a foe as it is for many of us. It is their friend. These individuals do not try to control the lives of others. They are not even trying to control their own lives. As illumined as they are, they don't know what is best for themselves, let alone what is best for others. They are not kings; they are servants: servants to others, to the earth, and to the cosmos. They are never alone, not only because they know their oneness with God, but because who they are includes us. They know them-selves to be a part of us, and therefore they accept us as we are, thus enabling us to become what we are capable of being.

We need these awakened ones, and the wonder is that all of us can be as they are. Imagine the power of a few of us when we are aware of the kingdom of God that is here. We have sensed the work of ones such as these. We know of others who are living simple lives and who are making a difference in the lives of people they touch each day. Imag-ine the power for good in a planet filled with millions of these people. This is God's plan, and we are an integral part of it.

Chapter Nine

Awake O'Sleeper

Awakenings

We wake up when we are ready and at a time we do not know. It is like the wind— *"...you do not know whence it comes or whither it goes, so it is with everyone who is born of the Spirit."*[1] For instance, we may awaken during times of crisis. Elijah, the prophet, was fleeing the wrath of Jezebel and was in a state of despair. He was ready for his life to end, but then on Mount Horeb, which means solitude, he heard the still, small voice. *...a great and strong wind rent the mountains, and broke in pieces the rocks...but the Lord was not in the wind; and after the wind an earthquake, but the Lord was not in the earthquake; and after the earthquake a fire, but the Lord was not in the fire; and after the fire a still small voice* (I Kings 19:11-12). Moses likewise experienced the Presence on Mt. Horeb. He was not troubled as Elijah, but his solitary life as a shepherd invited reflection and therefore a spiritual awakening. Buddha and Mohammed also found solitude to be conducive to their awakening, but the difference between them and Moses was that they were actively searching for God while Moses was at work. Charles Fillmore, co-founder of the Unity movement, yearned for God and vowed to "go to headquarters" under the premise that a relationship could be forged with the Creator. After about six months, the breakthrough occurred.

Spiritual awakening can be soothing and uplifting, or it can bring us to our knees. Saul of Tarsus, the one who became Paul, was jarred out of his narrow-mindedness when Jesus spoke to him on the road to Damascus. The event so confused Paul that he was blinded. This encounter changed Paul forever and altered the direction of his life. It was fourteen more years before his missionary journeys began, but the mystical experience on the road to Damascus was the root of the remaining years of his life.

In addition, remember that Simon Peter, the fisherman who became a fisher of men, was awakened by a question posed by Jesus, *"But who do you say that I am?"* Simon Peter awoke when the question was answered by the indwelling Presence Jesus called Father. So often we ask for answers when it might be more fruitful to ask for a question that will stir us and shake us from our slumber. These examples of awakenings tell us about the interior lives and mystical experiences of some of the most illumined people who have ever walked the earth.

Their lives illustrate that awakenings can occur in a variety of ways. We can be in despair like Elijah or alone and about our work like Moses. We can yearn for God as did Buddha and Mohammed, or we can be on a prideful, personal crusade like Saul of Tarsus. A question can call forth the presence of God that lies within us. The Presence is like the wind, we know it blows, but we do not know where it comes from or where it is going. Our spiritual birth can rock us as it did Saul or comfort us as it did Elijah. However, regardless of when and how we are spiritually awakened, it is God's grace that makes it possible rather than our efforts.

When It Comes

A spiritual awakening usually comes suddenly, but years of unconscious preparation lay the foundation for the initial stirrings of a person's spiritual nature. Often the individual has been introspective and therefore, at least, partially aware of a mysterious part of himself or herself that is seeking expression. In many instances, this spiritual self shows itself dimly through the desire for some earthly expression, but in reality something divine is moving to the surface of the soul.

I recall that as a child I had an inclination toward stillness, silence, and solitude. I used to sit alone by the sea and listen to the pounding of the surf or crawl into a thicket of bushes in the forest and rest quietly as the other children played nearby. This, of course, is not the normal state of a child who tends to be in constant motion until exhaustion or mother puts an end to the perpetual play that is the heart of a child's day. Now stillness and silence are the center of my life and the soul of the inner journey that has captivated me.

An awakening is often marked by a mystical experience or at least an uncommon experience that we do not understand. In fact, we can sometimes look back on our lives and see a series of events that moved us at the time they happened, but that we tried to discount as meaningless or weird occurrences. However, there is a part of us that knows this is not true. The sign is that we never forget what happened. We simply put it aside. Later, we recall the experience and come to understand it to be a piece of the puzzle that allows us to see our lives as a spiritual journey.

The Suffering Soul

Once a man was distraught while driving home from work. Tears clouded his vision, so he pulled off the road, placed his head on the steering wheel and sobbed. With his chest heaving and through the sounds of his own labored breathing, he heard a still, small voice say to him, "Stop struggling!" With these two words came a peace that passed understanding. This is the way God works, and only God can cause transformation with a few simple words. Any of us could have said to this man, "stop struggling," but there would have been little effect. He may have even resented our admonition. He might have known he needed to let go, but he was not able to do so. However, when God speaks, we listen. When anyone has a spiritual experience, an indelible mark is made on the soul.

In many instances, the awakening or life changing event happens during a difficult time, for when the soul suffers, it is often more receptive to the Divine and more sensitive to spiritual forces that reside within it. Tears and truth join together to transform us. As the story above illustrates, the actual experience can be simple and direct, yet profoundly moving.

The heart of the initial awakening is that we catch a glimpse of another world or way of life. The tearful man driving home from work discovered a peace that tran-scended circumstance. Sometimes we receive an insight into ourselves or a situation that allows us to see ourselves differently, to gain another perspective, or to respond with peace and compassion.

We may hear a voice, think a new thought, have a vision or a dream, write a poem, or be touched by feelings that are different from what we would ordinarily experience in a similar situation. For instance, Joann struggled with forgiveness. She wanted to let go of the hurt she suffered when a good friend betrayed her. Joann persisted, but after two years she still became angry when thinking of the hurtful situation. One evening in prayer and meditation, an insight came to her that healed her soul and freed her from resentment. The inner voice told Joann that since the time of the betrayal, she had grown. She may look like the same person, but inwardly she was different. Her persistence had helped to transform her and make her willing toward God. Because she had changed, she was no longer the person who was betrayed. In fact, who she was today had never been betrayed. This is the kind of new thought that an individual experiences when she is being transformed.

Ethan was an alcoholic who wanted to be free of his disease, but his greater desire was to be loved. The combination of his unwholesome search for love and his disease took him into the depths of despair. Not only was he estranged from most people around him, he also despised himself, and yet he wanted to be healed. He was willing to be healed. One night he sat alone in his apartment, drinking and feeling sorry for himself. A warmth began to build in the center of his chest. It became hard to breath. Ethan thought he was having a heart attack, but at the same time the warmth was strangely reassuring. He no longer felt alone. The warmth began to move from his chest into the other parts of his body. He felt loved. This was the beginning of his healing. A moment of being loved was enough. Ethan had been shaken from his slumber and was beginning to awaken spiritually.

The avenues of God's expression are many, but in each instance we truly hear or see. We know the meaning of the words, *"But blessed are your eyes, for they see, and your ears, for they hear"* (Mt. 13:16).

The Delectable Wound

A spiritual awakening shows us a new world and new way of being. The challenge is to live from this newly realized consciousness of the Presence. It lingers for a time, but it does not stay. We have caught a glimpse of the "way it is," but eventually, the vision fades. Its appearance was so quick and so mysterious that we do not know how to make it stay, nor can we.

For a few days, for a week, life is different. During this brief time, we think we will never return to our old way of reacting and being. Good riddance, we think! However, it does not take long to realize that we are not yet able to live continuously in and from this new consciousness. It is as though we are walking in a forest shrouded in a morning mist. Suddenly, the sun breaks through, and we see a beautiful clearing before us. We step forward, but then the mist returns, and we see dimly again. This is normal. Spiritual birth, like all births, is only the beginning. Now we must grow. Few people emerge from the womb of spiritual birth fully actualized and prepared to serve the One who gave them birth. There is sadness in the return of the mist, but we savor the taste of the new life and sense the new values that will determine our future actions.

Whether the initial event is mystical, pleasant, or jarring, the soul is wounded. The search for God and union with the Creator will soon be the central focus of our life. The hound of heaven is upon us, and although we may meander, our circuitous and torturous route eventually leads us to the One we seek. We understand the meaning of these insightful words from Francis Thompson's famous poem, "The Hound of Heaven."

> I fled him, down the night and down the days;
> I fled him, down the arches of the years;
> I fled him, down the labyrinthine ways
>   Of my own mind; and in the mist of tears
> I hid from him…[2]

But then the day dawns when we realize the revelation of the hound of heaven says:

> I am he Whom thou seekests![3]

As we seek God, God is always seeking us, and many of us feel this seeking as a kind of wound.

Two mystics in particular speak of this wound. In 1667 when Madame Guyon was nineteen years old, she went to a reclusive Franciscan friar who said to her, "Madame, you are seeking without that which you have within. Accustom yourself to seek God in your own heart, and you will find him."[4] The friar's word had a profound effect upon her. She said, "I felt in this moment a profound wound, which was full of delight and of love—a wound so sweet that I desired that it might never heal."[5] Saint Catherine of Genoa of the 15th century expressed a similar insight of a soul touched by God—"a wound of Unmeasured Love."[6] The wound is sweet and delectable because although it does not heal, it is the sign of the touch of the Divine. We now yearn for the One, and there is no desire for the yearning to cease. It is as if we know that we were created for the love of God. The intensity of the experience may wane, but the memory of what we have seen, heard, or felt never totally goes away. We may not speak to others about what happened to us, but the experience whispers in the quiet place of our inner being, "What you have felt was real; it is the way you are meant to live." Like a seed, the divinely initiated event rests within us ready to burst forth when we take the time to nurture it with our attention, wonderment, and gratitude. This kind of spiritual experience is a revelation of our divinity, our true self. It touches us deeply and paves the way for our complete transformation. However, spiritual awakening can also occur when we experience the depth of our humanity. Out of this darkness a great light can shine and the eternal call can be heard, Awake O'Sleeper.

Notes

1 John 3:8.

2 D. H. S. Nicholson and A. H. E. Lee, *The Oxford Book of English Mystical Verse.* First American Edition. Acropolis Books, Inc. Lakewood, CO 1917. 409.

3 *Ibid.*, 415.

4 Evelyn Underhill, *Mysticism.* E.P. Dutton New York, 1911. 184.

5 *Ibid.*

6 *Ibid.*, 196.

Chapter Ten

The Darkness Of The Cocoon

The Human Path

Light can show the way, or it can blind us. Saul, the persecutor of Jesus' followers, was blinded on the road to Damascus.

> ...*suddenly a light from heaven flashed about him. And he fell to the ground and heard a voice saying to him, "Saul, Saul, why do you persecute me?" And he said, "Who are you, Lord?" And he said, "I am Jesus, whom you are persecuting; but rise and enter the city, and you will be told what to do." The men who were traveling with him stood speechless, hearing the voice but seeing no one. Saul arose from the ground; and when his eyes were opened, he could see nothing...*
> (Acts 9:3-8)

The mystical experience showed him that his persecution of the Christians was in opposition to God's will. Saul's mental confusion physically blinded him, and he was cared for by Ananias, a follower of the Way and a man Saul would have imprisoned. Saul of Tarsus became the Apostle Paul, but for him, there was no light dissipating the mist in the forest. There was a blinding light that eventually helped him to see. His first sight was of his humanity and his false pride. He experienced but could not see Jesus, although eventually he saw his own error and arrogance. Initially, there was no peace; there was anxiety and bewilderment. The light that shined revealed the darkness of Paul's soul.

Often those with the strongest personal identities and egos awaken through despair. King David was awakened not because he saw his true self or caught a glimpse of his oneness with God, but because he saw clearly his humanity and its weaknesses. What he witnessed shook his world, and the result was that he drew closer to God.

David lusted after Bathsheba, the wife of Uriah, an officer in King David's army. David ordered Uriah to the battlefront and further instructed Uriah's fellow soldiers to retreat from him while the battle raged. In this way, Bathsheba's husband was slain, and David was able to take her as his own. Nathan, a prophet, came to David and told him a story about a man who unjustly took what was not his. The king was enraged, but then Nathan told David that he was the man in the story. David understood the prophet's message, and out of his anguish David wrote Psalm 51 in which he expressed his remorse and need for forgiveness. He asked for *a clean heart* and that *a new and right spirit* be placed within him. The need for forgiveness often accompanies a spiritual awakening.

The light of spiritual awakening reveals all things. It

can shine into the dark places and puzzle us as it did Paul, or it can bring greater clarity and a sense of mission as it did Buddha. The light of truth can reveal a need for forgiveness as it did David, or it can ignite a bush and reveal that the ground upon which we stand is holy ground as it did Moses.

Shaken From Our Slumber

Spirit has Its ways of shaking us from our slumber. Sometimes we are gently roused, at other times, we are rudely awakened. The good news is that Spirit calls everyone. Even those like David and Saul who have taken or would take the life of another are called to discover who and what they are and to make a contribution to the human family. It seems that when our humanness dominates our psyche, it is our humanity rather than God that we first see.

However, just because our awakening may begin with peace does not mean that we will be able to avoid looking at our humanity. When we are born physically, we grow in stature; when we are born spiritually, we grow in understanding of our humanity as well as our spiritual nature. We are born of water and Spirit, and it is our destiny to probe and explore the fullness of creation and the many dimensions of our being. Basically, we must face ourselves—the human and the divine. And it can be just as difficult to discover that we are spiritual beings as it is for us to realize that our whole life has been self-centered and without true meaning.

I remember when I first started reading the writings of the mystics. I discovered that many of them such as St. Teresa of Avila referred to themselves as wretched.

It is absurd to think that we can enter Heaven without first entering our own souls—without getting to know ourselves, and reflecting upon the wretchedness of our nature...[1]

This was in direct opposition of my understanding that we are people of sacred worth. I was repulsed by the word *wretched.* In fact, I nearly put aside the books I was reading, but then it dawned on me that these were some of the most illumined people who have ever walked the earth. Their lives were a closer walk with God. Why did they call themselves wretched? What were they trying to say? What did they understand that was unknown to me?

Finally, through God's grace, I began to understand. The spiritual experiences of the mystics revealed to them their true nature as children of God. However, they were also shown their humanity and its weaknesses. For them, there was a vast chasm between the truth of their being and their humanity. The good news is that people like St. Teresa also conveyed the wonder of who and what we are. Their rhetoric was a matter of their perspective at a specific time and the message they were trying to convey.

The lesson for me was that the spiritual path includes both our human and our spiritual natures. It is enlivening beyond words to experience the spiritual self that lives in oneness with God, but it is likewise helpful to fully experience the human self that thinks it knows best. Through our spirituality, we come to know love and our oneness with God, but through our humanity we realize the need for forgiveness, compassion, and humility. Through our spiritual self, we realize we can help others; through our humanity, we understand that we need help as well.

Soul Sadness

Sometimes our awakening floods us with feelings of joy and oneness. We feel a part of everyone and everything. We are worthy and acceptable to God. We are people of sacred worth. However, spiritual chronicles also record that we sometimes feel a profound sadness or melancholy. Nothing we have ever done matters. A kind of cosmic sorrow overcomes us. This is not the feeling that we have when someone tells us we are worthless. This lack of worthiness is because we are identifying with our humanity. This is where humility is born. This is crucial because the greater our humility, the greater the grace of God.

In 1952, Joel Goldsmith, a modern mystic, experienced a profound sense of failure. During this time, he wrote a letter to God dated November 18, 1952.

This past night has been a continuation of nightmares. For weeks now my soul has jumped back and forth between hope and despair, joy and anguish, doubt and confidence; but last night came the hell of the realization of separation from God. Today all ties with "this world" are broken. Today all concern for persons and events are gone...All hope for good here is departed, and I look forward to the unknown with a light heart.

This is the end of the road. From 1928 to 1952, I really tried—my life, my work, everything went into what I believed was a search for God and God's work. It is twenty-four years almost to the month, and it has been failure. Oh, yes, a glorious failure, not one to be ashamed of. This work is a failure only after twenty-four years of having honestly, earnestly, faithfully, lived up to the highest I knew or was capable of, twenty-four years of giving to the fight days and nights as complete a sacrifice of personal interests as has been possible. So if failure, I can at least glory in it.

There are no regrets. Since my best went into it, I cannot feel that had I done so and so it might have been different. Up to my understanding and capacity, I gave it all, and failed. So my failure is my triumph. I glory, glory, glory in a great failure, and if a failure it must be, rejoice for it is a grand and noble failure.

So having nothing left to place at his feet, here it is: take my failure. It is the only perfect thing I have to offer up. Take it, Father: a beautiful, perfect failure, a bright and shining failure. It is all I have, and it is Yours.

Your son,

Joel[2]

As Goldsmith emerged from this spiritual crisis, he received a gift of peace and a profound insight, "You can never succeed because God is the only activity, but you can be the instrument for God's work. You can be the instrument for God's labor; you can be the instrument for God's love, but nothing more than that." So the great lesson was borne home to him that he had failed because he had believed that he had the power to succeed or to fail when all he could be was the instrument for the hand of the Divine.[3]

This kind of soul sadness is not to be chased away with

song, friends, and good times. It is to be experienced because from it will come a willingness to be taught. We will give up needing to be right and having to know what lies ahead. We release the idea of personal power and accomplishment. Soon we will be able to place our hand in the hand of the unknown. Soon we will embrace the mystery of life. This is where and when faith is born. Many people believe that faith is nurtured by light like a plant that is nourished by the sunlight. This is not true. Faith grows when it is dark. Mystery and not knowing are the light and rain that cause the seed of faith to sprout and grow.

This is what happened to Paul. He was shrouded in darkness, and he began to trust. He heard the voice of Jesus, but he came to know the indwelling Christ that inhabits each of us. Eventually, Paul said, *"...it is no longer I who live, but Christ who lives in me"* (Gal. 2:20).

Every human being experiences difficult and challenging times. Only a few of us know that this darkness can be the darkness of the cocoon. Imagine how it must be for a caterpillar when it begins to retreat from the world that has been its home. The cocoon is formed, and darkness descends upon the creature. Just as an unseen force has willed the formation of the cocoon, so do unseen forces begin to reshape the worm's body. After a time, the butterfly emerges and takes flight. It once crawled upon the ground; now it soars above the earth and flutters from flower to flower. This well-known phenomena is one of the most profound transformations that happens in nature. We are in awe of the changes that take place. However, even this transformation is dwarfed by the transformation that happens when a human being awakens spiritually.

The key for us is to realize that all darkness can be the darkness of the cocoon. With assurance we let go and allow an unseen Presence and spiritual forces to reshape our lives. They ask us to let go of what we once valued, so we can receive new values. What once was is no more. There is no need to live as we once lived. Once we crawled or staggered through life; now it is time to soar.

Mystical experiences or happenings that point us in an unknown direction or cause us to question our values and purpose are best reflected upon. It was this way for Paul. Remember, it was 14 years after his road to Damascus experience before he began his work. We do not know specifically what he did during those years, but most likely he reflected not only upon what had happened to him, but upon his life. He must have questioned everything. He was passionate about life, but his passion had been misdirected. He had to discern the will of the One who had touched him deeply.

This is what we must do—reflect upon what has happened to us, the current direction of our lives, and the next step we must take. However, it is clear that no step is to be taken unless we are guided, unless we feel the hand of Spirit upon us. Then we act with boldness and daring. The shocking news is that often this guidance may seem absurd. We tend to think we have been called to some great work when the first clear guidance we receive might be to mow the lawn, read a book, take a walk, call a long forgotten friend, or travel to a distant place.

Brother Lawrence was a Carmelite monk who lived in the 17th century. He worked in the hospital kitchen of the monastery. At first, he despised his work, but eventually, he decided to do the simplest task for God. Brother Lawrence's

commitment to practice the Presence resulted in his
writing of "feeling joys so continual and so great tha.
scarce contain them."4 And the joy was not solely his.
People began to sense his bliss and peace. Church leaders
and individuals came far distances to seek his counsel and to
discover why he lived so immersed in God. Brother
Lawrence's ministry was not grand and impactful in the
conventional sense, but because it originated in and was
sustained by Spirit, it touched the lives of thousands of
people and continues to do so today.

One More Time

Sometimes our new life begins in darkness. Sometimes
it begins in light. If our awakening experience is a pleasant
one, the human tendency is to want to repeat it. We want a
confirmation that what happened was real. And besides, it
was pleasant—we want to feel loved again or to experience
the peace that caused us to weep. Joy may have been an
actual physical presence in us, and we want that feeling
again. This is our human tendency, but it is not to be. The
desire to experience the phenomenon again is an ego desire.
It is wanting what a loved one can give instead of yearning
for the loved one. The spiritual path rises above human
desire. It calls us to yearn for the One. The soul wound is
not for what Spirit can give us, but for Spirit Itself. Wanting to repeat the past keeps us in the past and unable to see
the next step we are to take. Yearn, but not for what happened. Yearn for God and be willing to fully experience
whatever happens.

After we catch a glimpse of the kingdom of God here on
earth and the wonder of the experience passes, we may try
to go back to our old way of living and behaving. The

difficulty is that what was once successful no longer works as it did, or it is no longer satisfying. We may curse what has happened. "I was happy before God touched me. Now I don't know what to do with my life. Nothing fulfills me anymore. I used to enjoy..., but now nothing brings me happiness."

We are out of the cocoon, but we have not yet taken flight. We are outside the darkness of the cocoon, but we stand in its shade. We may try to explain the happening away and push forward, but we never really do. The hound of heaven is always nearby.

An attempt to return to our previous way of being is a call for further cleansing and purification of our soul. The awakening showed us a new world, but it is still a foreign land because we are not ready to dwell there. A part of us wants to answer the call, but other parts of us are unwilling to make the required changes.

Jesus spoke of this part of the process of spiritual growth when He said,

> *"Then two men will be in the field; one is taken and one is left. Two women will be grinding at the mill; one is taken and one is left. Watch therefore, for you do not know on what day your Lord is coming."*
>
> (Mt. 24:40-42)

Many people believe that Jesus is talking about the rapture in which thousands, in fact 144,000 souls, will be taken to heaven. But this is not what he said. He spoke of two men and two women. One is taken, and one is left. I believe this is a reference to an inner process that occurs as the soul is purified. Certain thoughts, attitudes, and beliefs, symbolized by the men, are retained within the soul and other parts of us are left behind. Those left behind are not a part of our spiritual nature. For instance, close-mindedness, prejudice, and intolerance are left behind while humility, inclusiveness, and acceptance of others are attitudes of being that are a part of our spiritual nature.

This is also true of our feelings, symbolized by the two women. Feelings of condemnation, guilt, and unforgiveness must be left behind or purified from the soul. Love, compassion, and kindness are retained. The truth is this is no great mystery. It does not take long for an individual who is aware of his or her inner world of thought and feeling to know what needs to be retained and what needs to be left behind.

This process does not happen in a day. In fact, for most of us, the process is a long one. Paul spoke of dying daily. This is a reference to the inner process of soul purification and letting go. He soared to incredible spiritual heights by constantly letting go of what weighed him down, and as you know, his initial burden was immense. However, Paul's desire for God and willingness to serve combined with God's grace slowly and steadily purified his soul until the spirit of the One he once sought to discredit began to live in him. Paul eventually made the greatest discovery any human being can make—the indwelling presence of God. Paul called this God-presence the Christ, the hope of glory.

Friends, this is the darkness of the cocoon, the travail of birth. The soul suffers in anguish because it is giving birth to the presence of God. Part of us resists this birth and for good reason. Our whole life is about to change. And part of us rejoices because the soul is being true to its nature by fulfilling its ultimate destiny—giving birth to the image of

God. In this birth, there is pain not unlike what an athlete goes through as he or she prepares the body for some physical feat. In this instance, of course, the feat is a birth that is of great value not only to the individual, but to the world. Spirit has another avenue through which to touch the lives of others. This is the heart of the second coming.

Notes

1 St. Teresa of Ávila, *Interior Castle*. Translated and edited E. Allison Peers, Image Books, Doubleday and Company, Inc., 1961. 53.

2 Lorraine Sinkler, *The Spiritual Journey of Joel S. Goldsmith*. Harper and Row, 1973. 173-174.

3 *Ibid.*, 174-175.

4 Gene Edwards, editor. *Practicing His Presence Frank Laubach Brother Lawrence*. Christian Books, Goleta, California, 1973. 92.

Chapter Eleven

Preparing For The Second Coming

What Would You Do?

Masses of people believe the second coming will give rise to a world in turmoil—earthquakes, floods, famines, and wars. Non-believers try to ignore the prevalent religious beliefs about these end times while believers remind the unsaved of the doomsday prophecy in the hope that fear will bring these individuals into the household of faith. Of course, for thousands of years these four supposed portents of the return of Jesus—earthquakes, floods, famine, and war—have been with us. For this reason, in nearly every age, people believing in the imminent return have prepared for the worst.

How would you prepare for a plethora of natural disasters sweeping over the earth if you were convinced that they were coming in a few short months? Would you stockpile food and medical supplies? Would you acquire high powered weapons to protect yourself, your family, and your goods? Would you retreat to a secluded location and live primitively? Would such preparations be of any use if there was a literal second coming?

If you knew that difficult times were ahead for you personally, how would you prepare yourself? Many of us would gather our friends around us. People of vision and inner strength can fortify us during times of difficulty. The truth is that we face great challenges such as the death of loved ones or grave, life threatening illnesses. The good news is that friends do rush to our side. People we don't even know pray for us. We try to enlist the aid of the Almighty. We want to know that we are not alone, that God is with us.

I have asked myself what I would do if I knew that the world was nearing a time of upheaval or that I was entering a time of trial and tribulation. My hope is that such challenges would not alter my approach to life. Essentially, my hope is that I prepare for the mystery of the future by the way I live my life everyday.

The things we do and say either invite or delay our spiritual awakening. It is as Jesus said, *"The wind blows where it wills, and you hear the sound of it, but you do not know whence it comes or whither it goes; so it is with every one who is born of the Spirit"* (Jn. 3:8). Being born anew is God's blessing, and it is God's grace that determines the day. Obviously, this is a river we cannot push. We cannot make it happen, but there are things for us to do.

Adopting A Way of Life

Our spiritual awakening is a mystery, but we can adopt a way of life that invites the second coming. It begins with us examining our lives. Remember, it was Plato who said,

"The life which is unexamined is not worth living."[1] This a time for reflection. *The Third Coming* explores one of the most profound aspects of life. As you can tell, we are venturing to the core of life's meaning and purpose. It is time to ask the most profound questions or perhaps it is better to say that we imagine Spirit is asking us these questions. *What do you value? For what would you give your life? What kind of person do you want to be? What would you do if you knew you could not fail? What is the center of your world? What is the evidence that this is so?*

Notice that in our imaginary dialogue with God, God is not giving us answers or telling us what to do. Questions with great implications are being posed. It is our "hope of glory," the indwelling Presence that must answer.

Let these and other questions stir you. Answers may come, but what is most important is that you are stirred and moved by the questions. Life must be different because you heard the question. In this way, you are changed. This is a good beginning. A new you is being born, one more receptive to the coming birth.

Remember, this process is an inner one. No one is to be consulted for answers. Often the people with all the answers don't even know the question. No book of wisdom, not even the sacred literature of the world, is to be consulted now. Write to no wise person. Your answer must come from within. In this way, your life becomes worth living because you have examined it and found it to be mysterious and boundless.

Bring An Empty Cup

It is easier for children to enter the kingdom of God because they bring an empty cup to the fount of life. They

are curious and adventurous. They are humble and willing
to learn. This attitude of mind and heart invites the return
and the emergence of the image of God. Many of the
mystics adhered to supreme humility expressed through the
mystic motto, "I am nothing, I have nothing, I desire
nothing."2 At this time, we may not be able to utter such
words, but we can stand outside and look at a clear night
sky and acknowledge how little we know. Job was one who
was secure in his knowledge and understanding until God
began to question him.

> *Where were you when I laid the foundation of the*
> *earth?*
> > *Tell me if you have understanding*
> *Who determined its measurements—surely you know!*
> > *Or who stretched the line upon it?*
>
> *Have you commanded the morning since your days*
> *began,*
> > *and caused the dawn to know its place...?*
>
> *Have you entered into the springs of the sea,*
> > *or walked in the recesses of the deep?*
> *Have the gates of death been revealed to you,*
> > *or have you seen the gates of the deep darkness?*
>
> *Can you bind the chains of the Pleiades,*
> > *or loose the cords of Orion?*
> > > > (Job 38:4, 12, 16, 17, 31)

Children bring an empty cup to the fount of life, but we
are adults, so let us bring no cup, for no cup can contain

God. Let us bring our humble souls and our desire for the One. Let us just come.

Let us not bring the world and its needs or our own needs, but let us also realize that the world will accompany us. It will want to be the center as it has been for years. When needs press in upon us, it is best to entertain these unwelcomed guests with acceptance.

Many years ago, a woman under great stress called me. She was seeing lights and could not get them to go away. She contended with them and struggled with what she saw, but to no avail. I suggested that she stop trying to make the lights go away, that she simply observe them and accept their presence in her life. As her contention diminished, so did the intensity of the lights until finally they were gone, and she was free. Her freedom came through acceptance. This is what we must do when the world presses in upon us. We do not resist. We give attention to the once distracting thought, image, or feeling, and then we accept it. In this way, the world will lose its power, and we will be less prone to bring a cup filled with concern to our God. Such emptiness prepares the soul for the second coming.

Nothing So Like God As…

Meister Eckhart, a 13th century German mystic, said, "There is nothing so like God as stillness." Logic dictates that if we want to know God, we must be like the One. This is the message that the psalmist heard, "Be still and know that I am God…" (Ps. 46:10). Stillness seems contrary to the lifestyle of the twenty-first century human being. The truth is: it is contrary. This is the point. We are preparing our souls not for the next career move or to position ourselves for the next upward move in the stock market. We are opening ourselves to the Presence. Many things will be contrary to what we have done before.

Stillness asks us to deepen our sensitivity. We have selected what we would be sensitive to; now we are simply to be sensitive. We will become aware of a beautiful outer world that has been unappreciated and unknown to us, but more importantly our stillness and sensitivity will allow us to catch a glimpse of the kingdom of God that is within us and around us.

This requires stillness and watching. Jesus asked this of his disciples while he prayed in the Garden of Gethsemane. *"Watch with me,"* he said, but they fell asleep. We, too, will slumber, but we will try again. Let us begin with our physical world. Sit in the midst of nature and watch. Don't look at objects and things. Instead, look at light reflecting off leaves and the shape that shadows make on the ground. Listen for the sound of the wind in the trees and your own breathing. Notice that you are not alone. Tiny creatures and small animals are close at hand. As Henry Benton who wrote *The Outermost House* determined, the animals that share our world with us are "citizens of other nations."

Our observation of the world around us will lead us into the current moment, a place that can be foreign to many of us. From here, we can take note of our thoughts. We watch them without judgment. We do not label them good or bad. The thought simply is. It exists. We do not contend with it. Our lack of naming and labeling allows us to remain detached from the thoughts that move within our minds. However, we are sensitive to them, for they tell us something about ourselves.

Next, we watch for feelings. They are more subtle and are often hidden within our psyche. Stillness, watchfulness, non-resistance, and a non-condemnatory approach will call them out where they can be accepted as they are. Images may emerge of situations when we felt the feeling power-fully and determined that we never wanted to feel that way again. The emergence of this feeling and the recollection from the past is an opportunity for healing, and every healing prepares the soul for its awakening.

How Do I Love God?

Nothing prepares the soul for its spiritual birth like loving God. Most people want to be loved and they are, but they do not feel loved because they have not yet discov-ered that love is experienced when it is expressed, not when it is gathered to ourselves. This is why some people have said that God is a verb rather than a noun. It requires action.

I believe that love can grow between human beings when they spend time together. We support one another's interests and learn about the other person. Essentially, we become more interested in the other person than in our-selves. We give gifts to one another, but the greatest gift is attention.

These principles are likewise active as we develop a relationship with God that leads to a mystical marriage of profound oneness. First, we spend time together. Of course, God is always with us, but we are not always with God. Our focus and attention are elsewhere. Love begins as we give attention to Spirit. We may read what others have written about their journey of oneness with God, but basically we become still and listen. Listening is one of the great qualities of a lover. Only then does the lover know how to assist and support the beloved.

ᴈ Is To Live

ᴌᴛ is possible to consciously prepare for a spiritual awakening, but it is best if we dedicate ourselves to living a spiritual life. We examine our lives and listen for the profound questions that God asks every human being. We become sensitive to the world of form and to the inner realm of thought, feeling, and image. Because nothing is so like God as stillness, we too become still. And we consciously give the gift of attention to God. From this humble beginning, love will grow. These are simple acts, but each one will ask us to examine or to change our intent. As our intent, our reason for being, expands beyond ourselves, then we become candidates for the return because our world is now greater than the one into which we were born.

And so we live, and we wait, and we live again. There is peace when our world may be in chaos. There is joy in the simple things. Finally, we have found happiness. We are present and aware of the world around us and the world within us. Thanksgiving abounds. This ultimately is the sign of a soul prepared for its birth—it is joyful, thankful, and conscious, and the world is whatever the world will be.

Notes

1 Plato, *The Dialogues, Apology, Section 38.*
2 Evelyn Underhill, *Mysticism.* E.P. Dutton New York, 1911. 400.

Section Four

The Third Coming

Chapter Twelve

Something Wonderful
Is Going To Happen

The Engine Of Evolution

Many species of human beings have inhabited the earth.
Homo habilis, the first true human, lived about 1.5 to 2
million years ago. The more recent cro-magnon man
emerged only 30,000 to 40,000 years ago. Through the
evolutionary process, we are moving toward something
ordained by God. The tendency is to focus upon the
changes in our bodies, in our appearance, but something
more important is happening. We are awakening to our
spiritual nature.

Undoubtedly, environment is a factor in evolution. It
demands that we adapt or die, but we are also being pushed
from within. We have a destiny to fulfill. We have seen it
in the way the wayshowers lived. Once survival was the
driving force of our species. It was me versus you. If there
was conflict or a shortage of food, it was better that I live

than that you live. Such beliefs birthed an aggressive species driven by the fight or flight impulse. Obviously, this species still lives in today's world. However, for a wayshower, the issue was not his survival, but our survival. Our destiny is not to continue as we are, but to become aware of what we are.

There have been grand moments in our evolution. When we first rose from all fours and stood upright, we took a giant step forward. We could use our hands to construct and use tools. However, the most far-reaching breakthrough in our evolutionary journey was when one of us achieved consciousness. Instinct was no longer the sole source of our wisdom. Through cognitive thought, we reasoned, and the groundwork was laid for bursts of insight, intuition, and creativity.

I believe that consciousness is the engine of evolution. I cannot confirm it, but my intuition tells me that our changing consciousness actually rewrites our genetic code. Eventually, those behaviors that seem unnatural or difficult become a natural part of our way of living and being. Then they do not have to be learned. Imagine a world in which love and compassion are natural. They are the inclination and genius of every human being. Our instinct is the survival of all of us. These are some of the fruits of the third coming. It is why something wonderful is going to happen.

Is It Enough?

A seeker once asked the transformed Siddhartha what was the difference between him and Buddha. Buddha answered, "I am awake." The wayshowers were awakened beings. They appeared different from us, not in appearance, but in what they did and in the way they lived. They were evidence of an emerging new species. They were the fore-runners of what we are and what we are destined to express.

Is it enough that a person awaken spiritually, that the person experience the second coming? When this occurs in the life of an individual, peace, power, compassion, and creativity are released from within. The person is blessed and becomes a blessing to the world. But is this enough?

The answer is no. It is not enough that one person or even a thousand people become avenues of God's expression. The divine plan is that all of us become ambassadors of the Presence. This is the third coming.

The first coming is the birth of a wayshower. Through-out the ages and in various cultures, there have been those who awakened. They were seeds sown by the tree of life. Each of these seeds became a spiritual giant and a sower of seeds. Each wayshower departed from the earthly realm, but in several instances, it was predicted that there would be a return.

They do return, and they have returned. People have had encounters with various wayshowers, but more impor-tant is the fact that numerous individuals have awakened spiritually. This is the heart and soul of the second coming because now a person values the same things that the wayshower valued and strives to live according to principles and ideals taught and demonstrated by the One who showed the way.

In the second section of this book, we briefly traced the development of the second coming or return idea as it wove itself through development of religious and spiritual thought. Now we come to the third coming, which is not the awakening of one person, but the awakening of the human race. This is why the wayshowers came—so there will be millions of us, billions of us, all of us who become avenues of Spirit's expression.

I believe that this is part of the divine plan and that it is imperative. One of the compelling reasons is that the problems the human family faces are so immense that they cannot be solved unless we first awaken spiritually. There is no human solution. The challenges of our species require that we all awaken. This is the only way they will be solved. Poverty, for instance, has plagued humanity for thousands of years. We have the resources to solve this problem. There is no reason for 20 million children to die of malnutrition-related problems every year. An awakened species not only has the means to eradicate poverty from the world; it has the will and the wisdom to do it. When we awaken and the new species takes its place in the world, something wonderful is going to happen. A breakthrough of cosmic proportion will occur. So grand and far-reaching is our future that in our current consciousness, we cannot fathom it; however we can sense it. Intuitively, even logically, we know that a species of beings who are spiritually awake would be an incredible force for good in the cosmos.

Long ago one of our species became self-aware. It was a dramatic event that has recurred for millions of years. Now we are beginning to discover that the self we are aware of is greater than we think. The self is not solely an individual, but all individuals. And there is more. The self includes all living things, the earth that is our home, the sun to which the sunflowers pay homage, and the great cosmos of billions of galaxies. The new species lives in this greater universe.

Hear Ye, Hear Ye
And so we have evolved to the point where we can sense

the possibilities, not of the single self, but of the greater self. Something is possible, but it cannot be experienced or achieved by only one person. Even a wayshower cannot live alone in the splendor of what lies ahead. Our wise Creator has made us one with each other and furthermore has conceived a divine plan that reveals itself not to one person, but to all people.

It is as if a grand announcement is going to be made, but it cannot be told to one person or to small gatherings of people. Every ear must hear what the Creator will say, but the message will not be given until all of us are listening. So let us support one another's awakening.

The first coming was a gift to the world. It was God's gift to the human family. The second coming is a gift given to each of us. It is personal. Remember Jesus said, "Your Lord is coming." And then there is the third coming that results in a fully awakened species ready to learn of its Creator's message—a message that Spirit has waited for billions of years to give. This is why I say, "Something wonderful is going to happen."

Chapter Thirteen

The Doorway Of The Kingdom Of God

A World Without Fear

The second coming marks the emergence of a fearless being. Its concern is not for itself, but for the greater self that includes everyone. This is why soldiers fall on grenades, people jump into icy waters to save those in peril, and why doctors travel to distant lands to assist the victims of the outbreak of a deadly virus. When we forget ourselves for just a moment, a fearless one emerges, and we act courageously. Fearlessness is why an individual breaks new ground and does things that seem unimaginable to most of humanity.

A wayshower may walk on water or ascend into the sky, but his most remarkable deeds are his ability to turn the other cheek and his treatment of outcasts. This is what one spiritually awake, self-aware being can do. He or she may even start a new spiritual movement. Imagine what a race of awakened beings is capable of doing. To wonder about such things is to ponder the implications of the third coming and to take one step closer to a world without fear.

So What Lies Ahead?

No one can foresee the future, but we can determine where our tendencies are taking us. People who focus on our abuse of one another foresee a time of doom and destruction. Our inhumane behavior should concern us, but I do not believe it is prophetic to look at our human tendencies. The true prophets of the future are our spiritual tendencies. They tell us what lies ahead. Our spiritual tendencies enable us to look around the bend in the road. So let us ask the question, "What are the spiritual truths that govern our lives?" The answer is vital because truths point to our spiritual tendencies and to what we are capable of doing and being.

The single, most fundamental spiritual truth is a part of every major religion. The Jews declare, "The Lord God is one." The Muslims chant, "La ilaha illallah, There are no gods, but God." Today's metaphysicians often affirm, "There is only God." These and similar statements convey the fullness of God's presence. They lead to the conclusion that God is the great reality, and we are one with each other. Jesus expressed this truth when he spoke with his disciples.

> *"...for I was hungry and you gave me food, I was thirsty and you gave me drink, I was a stranger and you welcomed me, I was naked and you clothed me, I was sick and you visited me, I was in prison and you came to me." Then the righteous will answer him, "Lord, when did we see thee hungry and feed thee, or*

thirsty and give thee drink? And when did we see thee
a stranger and welcome thee, or naked and clothe thee?
And when did we see thee sick or in prison and visit
thee?" And the King will answer them, "Truly, I say to
you, as you did it to one of the least of these my breth-
ren, you did it to me."

(Mt. 25:35-41)

This is a message of profound oneness, our oneness.
Because we are made in the image of the eternal Creator, we
are without end. Our physical bodies may perish, but we
continue. Nothing can touch our spiritual essence. We
experience our deepest pain when we are not true to our
spiritual identity. We are united with one another and are
here to care for and to help one another. However, in spite
of these truths, people live in poverty, family members
abuse one another, nations war against other nations, and
people are alone or feel isolated and lonely.

It has been said that loneliness is the greatest human
tragedy and that it denies our oneness. I recall talking to a
family as we prepared for the funeral service of a beloved
wife and mother. The family members told me that she had
said that she did not want to die alone, and, in fact, not
only were the family members with her, but each person
was touching her as she died. Not everyone is so fortunate.

Oneness is mysterious, but it is derived from the greater
fundamental truth that *there is no god, but God.* However,
how many of us have experienced this truth? What is
required before our understanding of oneness can move
from the head to the heart and from an ideal that feels good
to a practice that ensures that everyone will die in the arms
of those who love them?

There is a sign that indicates spiritual truths are moving from the head to the heart and are nearing a time when they will not only be the pillars of the cosmos, but the foundation of our daily lives. The sign is silence.

The wayshowers came and planted in human consciousness the idea of oneness and that we are to care for one another. They revered life, did no harm, loved us, and taught that we are all people of sacred worth. All wayshowers lived and taught these same ideals, but from where did the truths come? Obviously, they came from God, but what was the door through which they entered? The answer is silence.

The Language Of The Centuries To Come

In the 6th century A.D., St. Isaac of Spoleto said, "Silence is the language of the centuries to come." The wayshowers knew this language. It taught them everything they taught us. Basically, these ambassadors of God took the time to allow the Presence to communicate with them and to transform them. Under a tree, in a cave, while tending flocks, and during ordeals in the wilderness, they listened and learned a new language—silence. They discovered its power and that it was a doorway to the kingdom of God.

Just as silence was the beginning for each wayshower, so silence is the first sign of the third coming. Most of humanity is unfamiliar with the power of silence. We consider it to be the absence of sound rather than the presence of God. In fact, many of us are so uncomfortable with wordless silence that it has become a counseling technique. The counselor says little knowing that the counselee will fill the void with his own words. Some of these words will hopefully contain insights into and answers to his problems.

Madame Guyon, a 17th century mystic, often sat in silence with her confessor, Father La Combe. Of this experience she said, *Little by little I started speaking to him only in silence, and at that point we understood each other in God, in an inexplicable, divine mode. Our hearts spoke and communicated a grace which defies words. It was a new country for him and for me, but so divine I cannot express it.*[1]

When we are in the silence together, we do more than communicate; we commune. For instance, I remember a fellow minister telling me that she sat at the bedside of a mutual friend while he died. Her dialogue with him was a silent exchange that was the prelude to his death. Silence, she said, invited the activity of God.

The truth is that silence is the womb from which we are spiritually born. Ghandi's stance of harmlessness, *ahimsa*, came not from the logic of his mind, but from the silence of his own soul. Mother Teresa's mission to be love in action to the poorest of the poor came from the silence. Every transcendent thought and insight have risen from the silence, and therefore from God, for silence is the doorway to the kingdom of God.

Fearlessness comes from silence. One moment we are trembling and afraid, and then the next moment we are willing to act boldly. Out of the seeming nothingness of silence comes every noble act and thought. From silence comes the expanded concept of self as a part of everyone. It is silence that teaches us we are a part of the earth and even the distant galaxies. Our ability to see beauty in people who appear repulsive rises from the silence.

Florence Nightingale had this vision. During the Crimean War, the wounded, sick, and dying were often left to die in hospitals. The smell of death was everywhere and agony filled the air. In the midst of this atmosphere of archaic medical practices, Nightingale carried a lamp and moved from soldier to soldier bringing hope and solace. It is said that some of those she cared for would kiss her shadow as she dispensed her care.[2] I have the feeling that such heroic actions occur not solely because we look beyond appearances to see the presence of God in another, but because we know that the person we minister to is a part of ourselves.

I can remember years ago being suddenly struck with the idea that every person is an altar at which I can worship. At first, there was nothing, and then there was this new idea. People have been illumined in exactly this same way since our earliest beginnings. First, there seems to be nothing, a void, silence, and then suddenly there is something new. And it is more than an intellectual idea. Silence, the language of the centuries to come, carries ideas to the heart, for it encourages us not only to think a new way, but to act in a new way. Out of silence comes the experience that makes things true for us.

Learning The Language

Personally, I am looking for evidence that silence is understood to be a doorway to the kingdom of God. In the future, I expect to hear fewer spoken prayers and to see more people listening. I also expect to see a period of frustration because listening is difficult. The mind is a wanderer. It often darts from one frivolous thing to another and dwells upon past hurts or future hopes and dreams. It seldom values the moment where the doorway to the kingdom hangs between past and future. Therefore, the first things we will hear will be the "sounds" of our own thoughts, feelings, and images. This is normal. Even Jesus encountered temptations when he listened. And it took Siddartha years before he awoke. And I wonder about Mohammed and the many nights he spent in the cave. It took time before he was ready to experience the night of power. Perhaps the burning bush was on fire on other days, but Moses did not have eyes to see it.

I believe silence calls us when we are young. It has been a natural part of my life since I was a child. I used to sit by the seashore and watch the waves and listen to the sound of the crashing surf. I did not know why I was there or what I was doing, but even when I was seven years old, I was comfortable listening and watching. Now before a meeting starts in my office, I sit in the silence for five minutes with the person I am meeting. When I have a difficult task, I sit in silence just prior to beginning the work at hand.

I know of a corporation that permits its workers to go to a "silent room" during the course of the day for contemplation and reflection. Perhaps the judge I know in North Carolina who begins his court with one minute of silence has learned the source of true justice. As more and more people experience the second coming, silence will be valued more and more.

St. Isaac was correct, silence is a new language to be learned. Through it we receive from the mind of God powerful insights, ideas, thoughts, feelings, and images. However, although in many ways silence is our natural language, we usually find it hard to listen. Just as our outer world is filled with more and more sounds, so is our interior world more and more accustomed to our own repetitious and habitual thoughts. To learn the new language, our attention must be turned from what we have known to what we do not know. Let us be willing to consciously walk from the light of what we think we know to the mystery and darkness of what we have never known. This walk of faith follows the footsteps of every wayshower who has gone before us. The good news is that when something emerges from the silence, it impacts us and gives us new eyes with which to view the world. The gift from the silence is more than a new idea; it is a motivating force that asks us to act.

Anyone who attempts to learn this new language will first have to pass through a place called acceptance. It will be necessary for the listener to learn to accept the unruly chatter of his mind. As long as we consider these thoughts, feelings, and images unacceptable, we will not be able to learn the new language. As long as we label them as negative, we will not hear the voice still and small. As long as we insist that they cease or change, the door to the kingdom will not open. This is the paradox. We accept the chatter of the mind, and then through the power of non-resistance, the chatter lessens, and we begin to learn the language of the centuries to come.

The Power Of Silence

As the third coming begins to dawn, silence will unleash the wonders of God's kingdom. Anyone who has experienced the second coming knows the power of silence. It is the doorway to the kingdom of heaven available to everyone. To not knock at this door is foolish. And so we stand at the door with the promise, *"...knock, and it will be opened to you"* (Mt. 7:7). Day by day our commitment to silence grows, and just as I am now encouraging you to learn to listen, so too will you encourage others to stand at the door and knock.

After the second coming comes and our spiritual awakening is underway, our prayers change. They are less about our problems and more about the experience of the Presence. A problem may be solved, but the soul yearns for God far more than for solutions to earthly challenges. As the third coming nears, more and more people will simplify their prayers. Knowing God will be enough. Central to our lives will be the opening of the door to the kingdom, so God's glory can be expressed. Personal retreats will allow for extended times of resting in the silence. It is amazing how uncentered we can become even when we practice listening daily. A three-day respite in a quiet setting reestablishes our equilibrium and renews our commitment to sit in silence. Once again, we know from experience that God is enough.

As more people experience the second coming, they will begin to listen. The relationship between a spiritual life and health, vitality, and wellness will become common knowledge. In the early 21st century, this revelation is occurring. Scientific studies are confirming that a spiritual faith contributes to healing in an undeniable way. Double blind studies conducted by medical doctors and researchers are reporting that prayer has a substantial impact upon the restoration of the body. It is interesting that often the patients do not know that they are being prayed for, and the people praying do not know the people who are in the study.

And still God's work is done. Why? Because the doorway to the kingdom opens. Mysteriously, through grace, changes take place. These are the signs of the birth pangs for the third coming, the spiritual awakening of the race.

It may take longer, but silence is destined to permeate

the business community. Think-tanks and their processes have been part of the university system for years. We have known for years that "two heads are better than one." Anyone trying to solve a problem knows it is often helpful to talk to other people about the challenge, but it is likewise important to spend time alone in contemplation. Through the creative process, we discover that divine intelligence makes itself known suddenly and through various means. We rest quietly, focus our minds with the understanding that there is an answer, and wait in silence. Then through images, dreams, thoughts, and ideas we begin to build a new world.

An awakened business community will understand these principles and put them to the test. Perhaps the leading indicator that this is rooted in the third coming is the fact that the motivation will not be increased profits, but an experience of the creative process itself, a desire to serve one's clients and customers, and a willingness to think as we have never thought before. Silence will remake the business community and something wonderful will emerge.

And then one day we will be ready for the breakthrough. Perhaps there will be something that impacts or threatens us all. Maybe there will be a regional conflict with a potential nuclear aftermath. Negotiations will fail. Diplomats from the global society will withdraw. In today's world, the leadership of technologically superior countries might exercise the military option of endless bombing in the hope that it will break the resolve of the combatants. This time, because the awakening of the race is at hand, another approach is taken.

We, the people of the world, cease our usual work and daily activities. Billions of us are silent, we listen. We pray

not for world peace, but that we are peaceful. Peace enfolds
the earth and the combatants, even as they strike out at one
another. Our silence is an invitation for the door to open.
And it does. Something wonderful happens. Hardened
hearts soften, and we have more than a tense time in which
armed conflict ceases while hostile thoughts and emotions
increase. We have peace. Thousands of years of *an eye for
an eye and a tooth for a tooth* dissolve in the consciousness of
God's peace that emerges from the kingdom. We now
know the power of silence and what it can do. The language thought to belong to the centuries to come now
belongs to us.

Notes

1 Piero Ferrucci. *Inevitable Grace.* Jeremy P. Tarcher, Inc.,
1990. 145.
2 *Ibid.*, 90.

Chapter Fourteen

No More Holy Wars

Silence Reveals Light And Darkness

Silence, the door of the kingdom of God, prepares us for the next step in our personal spiritual awakening as well as the global awakening that is our collective destiny. Silence shows us our souls—its light and its darkness. We see the truth of our being and the beauty that resides within us, but we are also shown our mistakes and parts of us we have never known or parts of us that we have known and never wanted to know again. We want to shun the darkness in ourselves, but if this is not possible, we want to change it. Spirit has another plan.

Our Creator asks us to come fully alive by experiencing and then accepting our mistakes, insecurities, guilt, and a host of other expressions of our humanity. We are asked to join the Creator in accepting ourselves just the way we are. This has been God's work for millennia. It is love in action. Now the call is for us to accept the unacceptable parts of ourselves that we have tried to hide. We must learn that the parts we fear have no real power over us. As we experience them rather than try to rid ourselves of them or change them, we learn of their powerless nature.

Acceptance helps us feel God's power in us. The result is peace. We have overcome a difficult challenge—accepting ourselves the way we are. Now we are capable of accepting other people and their mistakes. Now we are able to contribute to the spiritual awakening of the human family. We have trod the path of the wayshowers who learned to accept their humanity, so they could express their divinity. This is why they loved us unconditionally: not solely because they knew that within us was what we treasured in them, but because they accepted our humanity just as they had accepted their own.

Oneness Through Diversity

Oneness is a fundamental truth of the universe, therefore the spiritual tendency must be to discover and experience our oneness. The forces and pressures of the cosmos drive us gently, and not so gently, toward this divine intent. Acceptance is a necessary step along the way because unless we accept our differences we will not be able to experience our oneness. This brings us to diversity.

I believe our diversity, our many differences, is part of the divine plan. We are intrinsically one, but at the same time, we are diverse. We are male and female, our skin color is different, we worship God under the banner of many religions, sexual orientation is varied, and we eat different foods. The people of some cultures are somewhat stoic while others express themselves freely and emotionally. Only by accepting these many differences will we be able to experience our oneness. And our oneness is crucial because the wonderful things that are destined to happen cannot happen as long as we condemn or merely tolerate one another.

Silence leads us to acceptance because until we accept the unacceptable parts of ourselves, we cannot experience the full potential of the silence or witness the opening of the door of the kingdom of God. People who accept themselves lead the human family in accepting its differences. This is the path to the experience of our oneness. It is part of our journey to the third coming.

No More Holy Wars

We share a common spiritual identity, but we come to understand and then experience this oneness through accepting and experiencing our diversity. Oddly enough, religion often perpetuates non-acceptance and in some cases endorses condemnation. Religions have drawn lines in the sand that separate rather than circles that include everyone. And the lines have become holy wars. Generations of believers have followed the lead of the religious remnant of the spirituality of the wayshowers, and an *eye for an eye* becomes the cry of each new generation as it visits enmity upon those it does not understand.

This is why people turn from religion. Intuitively they know that these actions are inconsistent with the message. The purity of the teachings of the founder has been lost and in its place is a mutation. Numerous wars have been fought in the name of religion. The combatants would say in the name of God, but this is not true. There is no war in God, no taking of life. Today religion remains at the heart of conflict, skirmishes, and wars. Weapons are drawn and people lose their lives, but there is another kind of holy war that has raged every day for thousands of years. Even during the few years that there has been peace on earth, this war was waged. I have a feeling that if this war ceased, we would find a way to put down our weapons because a consciousness of compassion would be unleashed in the world. This is the holy war waged by religion against women. Why is it that women are not able to be ordained in many faiths? Why is it that a woman has never led one of these denominations? Are we not all spiritual beings with the same capacity for love, wisdom, good judgment, and compassion?

Remember that the spiritual birth of the individual opens the heart, and the soul becomes more intuitive, sensitive, and compassionate. The third coming, the spiritual awakening of the human race, will follow the same path. The balance of male and female will herald the third coming. Finally, men will cease blaming women for their feelings of lust and take steps to deal with their own feelings and insecurities. We will stop viewing women as their bodies or as weak and begin to see them as equal expressions of God.

I foresee the global ordination of women, and women serving as the leaders of their denominations. It is not that women will or should dominate the religious communities where they have been limited in their ways of service as much as it is time for balance. When the holy war against women ends, I believe there will be less war on our planet. Never has there been a time when men and women have stood as equals; therefore we have denied ourselves their leadership and the feminine consciousness that has been needed for thousands of years.

I look for this sign—men and women in unity together. When it occurs, we will be in the midst of the third coming. It is interesting that strides are being made in the business and governmental arenas, while religion remains the last bastion of non-acceptance for over half of the world's population and for the ones who have given birth to us all. Just as an individual cannot fully express his or her spiritual nature until both the thinking and feeling natures are activated, so the world cannot experience its spiritual destiny until men and woman stand as equals in all areas of human endeavor. The good news is that when the holy war against women is no more, the children they bear will become the most compassionate people who have ever walked the earth. This is because they will be children of the third coming.

Touching The Untouchables

Throughout history nearly every culture has had its untouchables. They are outcasts, considered to be the dregs of society. When we see them, we look beyond them as if they do not exist, or we glare at them as if to ask why they exist. They look at us with contempt or with humility and say, "I'm human. I have rights. I deserve respect." I wonder if they are not God's emissaries, for their message seems to be, "Won't you accept me just the way I am?"

As I write this chapter of *The Third Coming*, I believe that homosexuals are the current "outcasts" of the world. In the United States, the defender of freedom, discrimination based on a person's sexual orientation is permitted. Furthermore, this discrimination is allowed in a society that uses sex or sexual connotation to sell everything from automobiles, beer, perfume, clothes, and chewing gum.

Just as women have been the target of a holy war, so has the gay community found itself in the crosshairs of religion. Just as the balance between men and women will be a breakthrough heralding the third coming, so will the acceptance of the supposedly unacceptable be an equally powerful breakthrough in the coming days.

It may be that the breakthrough will begin with a challenge to discrimination in the military. Perhaps a case will be brought before the Supreme Court and found to be unconstitutional. No decision by a court, even the highest court in the land, can change the minds of its people, but the decision can indicate that the consciousness of the people is changing. If the Supreme Court rules against the discrimination of homosexuals, it will mean that the collective consciousness of America has ruled that this form of discrimination shall not be.

Currently, the gay population is under fire. The line has been drawn and harmful words and acts are prevalent, but eventually they will end. I don't know if the end of this holy war will be a breakthrough that calls for the third coming, but it may be. However, I know this: when we reach out to touch and include the people who most of the world finds unacceptable, whoever they might be, we will feel the hand of God upon us, and the third coming will be one day closer.

Breakthroughs are necessary in many areas. Some may serve as preludes to our spiritual awakening. Others may come as the result of the spiritual birth of millions of us. For instance, we need a justice system that is not penal in nature. Rather than being punished, our lawbreakers should be given the opportunity to experience the light and the darkness of their souls. In addition, hundreds of millions of our human family live in poverty. Every generation has had its poor. It is obvious that only a spiritually awake world can solve this problem, and my sense is that compassion will lead the way. The resources are available. The next step is the emergence of the fearless one who can forsake its need for protection and who is willing to share the world's resources with those in need.

A Simple Path

The path is simple, although it has been obscured for thousands of years. Silence leads to the experience of the Presence which unleashes our spiritual tendencies. In order to fully experience the gifts of the silence, we learn to accept ourselves and then others. We seek to understand rather than to be understood. This brings justice.

Women are liberated and their inclusion into the inner sanctum of the religious community gives birth to a new consciousness of compassion that helps to eliminate conflict and war. Actually, this new consciousness will not permit war to be waged.

The world's untouchables are touched. Today, it is the gay community. In the past, there have been many opportunities to reach out, but we were not ready. Not only were we not ready to touch the untouchables, we were not ready to awaken. Now I believe the rebirth is underway.

It is only a matter of time before we turn our attention of those who have little. Their need is a gift they give to us. Only a world that has experienced the third coming can receive the gift of need and ensure that every one has the opportunity to live a healthy, productive, love-filled, and joyful life. And finally, we will turn our attention to those who turned against us—those in prison.

These challenges are immense. Throughout our history, no society or generation has solved these problems. One of the central reasons is that the holy wars, poverty, and those discriminated against are not seen as opportunities for our collective breakthrough. In the past, we have tried to solve these problems, but they remained. They remained because only a new species is able to hear and heed the guidance that will show us the way.

Chapter Fifteen

In The Twinkling Of An Eye

One By One?

How will the earth become the womb of the new species? How will the spiritual awakening of the human race take place? If the second coming is personal and the rebirth occurs one person at a time, will thousands of years pass before the third coming? In the past millennia, how long did it take before we evolved into the next species that could carry us toward our spiritual destiny?

It may be that we march toward the third coming one by one, or it may be that other forces and processes are at work. Perhaps a crisis is necessary. We awaken or we die. Humans have adapted over time. We have changed or perished when there were changing conditions. It seems that those species who stood their ground and would not or could not evolve are no more.

Crisis can be the impetus for an individual to change and be transformed. All of us have felt the need to be made new. Basically, choices were presented to us. Our response to them revealed our values and character. As we became better human beings, our choices encouraged our spiritual tendencies to surface and to take their rightful place as the ruling force of our lives.

Other Forces At Work

Jesus said, *"For where two or three are gathered in my name, there am I in the midst of them."*[1] Whenever at least two people are united in a spiritual purpose, something greater than the two of them is present. This is the principle—the whole is greater than the sum of the parts. A mundane example of this idea is an automobile. Imagine all the parts of your automobile lying on your driveway. Not even an o ring or bolt is missing; however you do not have a vehicle of transportation. The good news is that when the car is assembled you have something greater than the sum of its parts. You have a way to travel from place to place.

When at least two people are united in a wholesome purpose, something greater than the two of them emerges. Some scientists know this principle because they work in teams as they seek to uncover the mysteries of the universe. Imagine how many times universal mind emerged as the scientists and engineers sought to put a man on the moon. This is the wonder of the Greek philosopher, Archimedes, who declared, "Eureka," I've found it! This is how astounding things happen.

The Apostle Paul apparently discovered a spiritual principle that could cause a dramatic change in the world and in people's lives. He wrote in I Corinthians, *Lo! I tell you a mystery, we shall not all sleep (die), but we shall all be changed, in a moment, in the twinkling of an eye...For this perishable nature must put on the imperishable, and this mortal nature put on immortality.*[2] Imagine the human family suddenly changed, elevated in consciousness in a way that releases the power of God upon earth and in the cosmos.

In the 1980's, a story dubbed the hundredth monkey was being passed from one spiritual group to another.

> The Japanese monkey, *Macaca fuscata*, has been observed in the wild for a period of over 30 years. In 1952, on the island of Koshima scientists were providing monkeys with sweet potatoes dropped in the sand. The monkeys liked the taste of the raw sweet potatoes, but they found the dirt unpleasant.
>
> An 18-month old female name Imo found she could solve the problem by washing the potatoes in a nearby stream. She taught this trick to her mother. Her playmates also learned this new way and they taught their mothers, too.
>
> This cultural innovation was gradually picked up by various monkeys before the eyes of the scientists. Between 1952 and 1958, all the young monkeys learned to wash the sandy sweet potatoes to make them more palatable. Only the adults who imitated their children learned this social improvement. Other adults kept eating the dirty sweet potatoes.
>
> Then something startling took place. In the autumn of 1958, a certain number of Koshima monkeys were washing sweet potatoes—the exact num-

ber is not known. Let us suppose that when the sun rose one morning there were 99 monkeys on Koshima Island who had learned to wash their sweet potatoes. Let's further suppose that later that morning, the hundredth monkey learned to wash potatoes.

Then it happened!

By the evening almost everyone in the tribe was washing sweet potatoes before eating them. The added energy of this hundredth monkey somehow created an ideological breakthrough!

But notice. The most surprising thing observed by these scientists was that the habit of washing sweet potatoes then spontaneously jumped over the sea—

Colonies of monkeys on other islands and the mainland troop of monkeys at Takasakiyama began washing their sweet potatoes!

Thus, when a certain critical number achieves an awareness, this new awareness may be communicated from mind to mind. Although the exact number may vary, the Hundredth Monkey Phenomenon means that when only a limited number of people know of a new way, it may remain the consciousness property of these people. But when there is a point at which if only one more person tunes-in to a new awareness, a field is strengthened so that this awareness reaches almost everyone.[3]

This is a remarkable story that reveals a principle of change that I speculate manifested itself during the fall of the Berlin Wall. In Germany, the consciousness of freedom was building. Around the world for years, prayers and thoughts focused on the demise of the wall. Then on December 31, 1986, millions of people united in peaceful thought and prayer. I have a poster in my home that depicts the world with that date inscribed below it.

The day came about because Jan and John Price of the Quartus Foundation sent out a call for a united consciousness. No one will ever truly know, but many people speculate that the wall began to develop "cracks" on December 31, 1986 that culminated in November 1989 when the wall was breached and freedom flowed from the hearts of the Berliners into the streets of Berlin. It was in that month that the wall ceased to be a barrier to the people of Germany. In scientific terms, we might say that a critical mass was reached after which the energy of freedom was released.

To Burn Like A Thousand Suns

Five billions years ago, the gas of a nebula began to collapse under the force of gravity. Eventually, it grew hot enough for hydrogen atoms to be fused into helium. A critical mass was reached, a chain reaction began, and our sun was born. Since that time the force of gravity and the energy of the nuclear fusion have balanced one another, and the sun burns with its own light.

People can reach a moment of critical mass followed by massive transformation in which they burn with their own light. Buddha, Moses, Jesus, and Mohammed, for instance, burned with a divine light. History records times of sudden transformation. Paul was first blinded by the light, but then the light was ignited in him, and he carried a message of truth to the world. One moment Moses was a shepherd, and in the next he was commissioned to lead his people to freedom. Buddha, Jesus, and Mohammed each awakened in a moment—Buddha beneath a tree, Jesus after 40 days in the wilderness, and Mohammed in a cave.

Everyone who has experienced spiritual awakening resonates with a divine vibration. It is as if a tuning fork is struck and those who are receptive can feel the vibration. Imagine a vibration so strong that all of us can sense it. This is the third coming

I believe that sudden shifts in awareness happen regularly around the world. Perhaps you have been at a meeting where there was great deal of contention and negativity. Suddenly, someone who has been quiet stands and voices another viewpoint that creates an opening where people can join together. Another person sees the possibility and speaks in support of the proposal. Now two are gathered and a positive energy begins to build. Something greater is emerging from some unknown place.

The dark curtain was rent, and creativity came. In this moment, it may be said that the people were of one accord. Blows could have been struck, but instead a cord was struck. A new vibration fills not the air, but the hearts and minds of those present.

This must have happened when the foundation principles of the Declaration of Independence were debated and then adopted on July 4, 1776. And remember Pentecost... the disciples were gathered in one place. I venture to say that the place was not simply a location, but a unity of mind and heart. In the upper room, on past days they had united in prayer.

All of these with one accord devoted themselves to prayer, together with the women and Mary the mother of Jesus, and with his brothers.4

Now on Pentecost, they were united again.

And suddenly a sound came from heaven like the rush of a mighty wind, and it filled all the house where they were sitting. And there appeared to them tongues as of fire, distributed and resting on each one of them. And they were all filled with the Holy Spirit...5

This is what happens when two or three gather together for a spiritual purpose. Spiritual forces are released from within them. Something greater than the sum of the people is present. Throughout history, this process has repeated itself. again and again, and for the most part has gone unnoticed by humanity. It is this process that enables groups of people to do incredible works that bring into manifestation the will of God. It may be that such a process will transform the human family on a global scale and show us our imperishable nature. We have only to be of one accord and to gather in one "place." Our physical place is planet earth, our cosmic home, but our gathering place is a willingness to become aware of the presence of God. Then shall the doorway of the kingdom of God be opened, the third coming will come, and the new species will be born.

In The Twinkling Of An Eye

An urban myth tells of an African American woman in court. A racist teenager killed her twelve year old son. The evidence is overwhelming, so the defendant's lawyer has placed the murderer on the stand to tell of his life in the hope that he will receive life in prison rather than the death penalty. At first the teenager is composed and speaks about his life without emotion, the same emotionless state he was in when he pulled the trigger and killed the woman's child. But when he says that no one wanted him, that he had no mother, he begins to cry. With shoulders heaving, and through genuine sobs of remorse he says how sorry he is for his actions. His only excuse is that no one wanted him, and that he had no mother. Only his muffled sobs can be heard in the courtroom.

Then a voice brimming with gentleness, love, and compassion fills the space created by the teenager's personal testimony. "I will be your mother." The people in the room turn in the direction of the voice. Astonished, they see the mother of the dead child rise and face her son's killer.

"I will be your mother. Until I die, I will be your mother. My son is gone, and so I ask you, will you be my son now?"

The teenage raises he head and asks in disbelief. "You want me to be your son?"

A simple yes escapes her lips, and he begins to cry again, but now he is not alone. The judge wipes away a tear and looks upon the reddened eyes of the prosecutor and the boy's lawyer.

The five words, I will be your mother, have transformed the courtroom and the lives of those present. And the hate that was in the racist's heart is no more. In its place is his answer to her question, "I will be your son."

No One Shall Be Left Behind

Some things are natural. As a speaker I have often stood before an audience and cried. In most instances, the people

did not know why I was crying. In fact, usually I did not
know why I was crying. The amazing thing was that the
audience joined me. A cord must have been struck, and
suddenly, in the twinkling of an eye, we were of one accord.
I conclude that it must be normal to join in the oneness of
tears.

Acts of great courage and sacrifice touch us. It is as if
we know that such acts are natural. They are destined to be
the norm rather than the exception. The third coming, the
spiritual awakening of the human family, is natural. It is
our destiny. It began when the tree of life cast its first seed.
This was the first coming. This is God's way, for all people
must have a wayshower, and each wayshower must simply
show us the way. When we follow the path that they trod
and live the life they taught us to live, it is as though the
wayshower has come again. This is the second coming, the
spiritual awakening of a human being.

Jesus told a parable of the shepherd who left his flock to
find the one sheep that had strayed. Surely, if a shepherd
will not leave behind one of his flock, our God will not
forsake even one of us when the new species is born. Amazingly, mercifully, our wise Creator has devised a way in
which all of us can be transformed.

Even now we march toward a critical moment. Whenever two or more of us gather for a spiritual purpose, we are
closer to the moment. Every act of loving compassion
prepares the way for the third coming when we will all
awaken. The new species will be born, and we will burn
with our own light, the light of God. For ages it has been
one light, one awakened being, and then another. One
person saying, "I will be your mother, will you be my son?"
But soon, what happened in the hearts of those in the urban

myth will happen in every human heart and each of us will burn with the light of a thousand suns.

Notes

1 Matthew 18:20.
2 I Corinthians 15:51-53.
3 Ken Keyes, Jr. *The Hundredth Monkey*, Vision Books, 1982. 11-17.
4 Acts 1:14.
5 Acts 2:2-4.